Prophetic Development

Prophetic Development

Insights to maturing in the Prophetic Anointing and Its Flow

By Dr. John A. Tetsola

End Time Wave Publications

Prophetic Development

Insights to Maturing in the Prophetic Anointing and Its Flow

Copyright© 2001 by Dr. John A. Tetsola. First printing. Printed and bound in United States of America. All rights reserved. No portion of this book may be reproduced in any form or by any means, including information storage and retrieval systems, without written permission from the publisher, except by a reviewer, who may quote brief passages in a review. Published by **END TIME WAVE PUBLICATIONS**, P.O. Box 141, Bogota, New Jersey 07603-0141.

ISBN 1-889389-21-8

Unless otherwise indicated, all Scripture quotations are from the King James Version of the Bible. Scripture quotations marked (NIV) are taken form the HOLY Bible, NEW INTERNATIONAL VERSION ®, Copyright © 1973, 1978, 1984 by International Bible Society. Used by permission of Zondervan Publishing House. The Amplified New Testament, Copyright © 1954, 1958, 1987 by The Lockman Foundation. Used by permission.

Those marked (NASB) are from the New American Standard Bible, Copyright © 1960, 1962, 1963, 1968, 1971, 1972, 1973, 1975, 1977 by The Lockman Foundation, La Habra, California. Used by permission.

Verses marked (TLB) are taken from The Living Bible, Copyright © 1971. Used by permission of Tyndale House Publishers, Inc., Wheaton, Ill. 60189.

Note: In some Scripture quotations, italics and quotation marks have been added by the author for emphasis only.

Table of Contents

CHAPTER 1
Sources of Receiving Prophetic Revelation   1

CHAPTER 2
Prophetic Interpretation and Understanding   85

CHAPTER 3
Growing in the Prophetic Anointing   99

CHAPTER 4
The Ways of Delivering Prophetic Words   111

CHAPTER 5
Guidelines for Prophetic Ministrations   123

CHAPTER 6
Positioning Yourself for the Prophetic Word   131

CHAPTER 7
Understanding the Transference of Prophetic Words of Promise to a Generation   141

CHAPTER 8
The Day After the Word of the Lord is Released   169

CHAPTER 1

SOURCES OF RECEIVING PROPHETIC REVELATION

No two people are exactly the same. We all have the same basic design, but under no circumstances do we feel, reason, act or think in the exact same way. We are unique expressions of God. This uniqueness is often seen in the way we respond to outward stimuli. For example, three different people might attend a musical concert and have three different reactions. The first person might find the experience uplifting because of the refreshing rhythm of the music. The second might be irritated by the beat and volume of the music and hear nothing but loud noise. The third could be so touched by the words of the song, that he or she is oblivious to the music. They all heard from the same source but received and responded differently.

The same is true of the spiritual realm. The way we receive from God varies according to the uniqueness of our personality, emotions and spiritual make-up. The truth is,

Prophetic Development

God didn't create Christian clones who respond as pre-programmed robots. Instead, He created us divinely distinct, as independent life forms who hear from the Creator on different spiritual frequencies. Because we are unique in this reception, we have the freedom to interpret incoming revelations in a way that is compatible with our understanding.

The principle of reception and interpretation is much like radio broadcasting and receiving. A radio tower transmits energy in the form of radio waves. When these waves arrive at a receiving antenna a small electrical voltage is produced. After this voltage has been amplified, the original information contained in the radio waves is retrieved and presented in an understandable form– the sound that comes from a loud speaker, a picture on a television, or a printed page from a teletype machine.

The same principle also applies to prophetic reception. The Spirit of God is like radio waves that carry vital information. As believers, we are the receiving antenna awaiting a signal from heaven. Therefore, whether we know it or not, we all receive prophetic transmissions from God, which are then translated into different forms such as visions, dreams, impressions and many other ways.

Sources of Receiving Prophetic Revelation

The form this information takes depends on the specific equipment within our spiritual house. That is, the frequency we are tuned in to and the position of our antennae. Since we receive in different ways, it would be foolish to stereotype the way Christians hear and receive from God. Remember, the way we interpret prophetic communication is not the standard for everyone. We should never expect others to operate exclusively on our particular frequency or understand completely the way God communicates with us. Now let's look at some of the ways we receive prophetic revelations.

MENTAL PICTURES OR IMAGES

The first way we receive prophetic revelation is through mental pictures. These pictures are much like the images seen in the subconscious mind while dreaming, yet they come while we are awake. They are clearer than dreams, but not as vivid as visions, lying somewhere between the realm of natural eyesight and conscious thought. They are often referred to as seeing with the mind's eye.

Many times, mental pictures come without warning or forethought. In the same way that a camera's eye momentarily opens to capture a particular scene, the mind's eye gives us snapshots of past, present and future images. In a split second, things can be perceived that are unrelated to one's present state of mind. These pictures can come in technicolor or black and white, in clear form or in abstract images.

A lot of Christians have experienced mental pictures at one time or another. In some cases, these pictures pertain to the every day, ordinary matters of life. In other instances, they are a bit less common. For instance, people have mental pictures of unexpected guests ringing their doorbells prior to their actual arrival. They have also seen in their mind's eye a telephone ringing only seconds before it actually occurs. Others experience mental flashes relating to matters of greater importance, such as imminent danger, political and social changes or even devastating weather patterns.

Whether these pictures seem important or insignificant, remember there are many dangers associated with the process of receiving and interpreting the meaning and source of mental pictures. Upon perceiving an imminent catastrophic event such as an earthquake, flood or even an accident, what must we do with it? How can we discern its origin? Is this mental picture from God? Is it an aberration of the mind? Or is it negative imagery sent by the devil?

Sources of Receiving Prophetic Revelation

These answers depend upon your spiritual position in Christ. If we truly believe that we have the mind of Christ, then we need to confidently explore the possibility that these images may have actually been given to us by God. Not every mental picture is from God. Again, it depends on the spiritual state of mind to be able to discern if it is from God or not. If we are uncertain about the spiritual state of our mind, then we must disregard these images until a time when we are confident that we are operating with the mind of Christ.

INTUITION AND IMPRESSIONS

Another way of receiving prophetic revelation is by intuition and impressions. Intuition has been described as knowledge that is arrived at spontaneously, without conscious steps of reasoning or inquiry. The expression, "I have an impression from the Lord," is Christian rhetoric that is similar in meaning to intuition but different in theory and application. For many Christians, the two are synonymous. For others, they are quite different.

Throughout our lifetime, we receive thousands of intuitive thoughts. No one is exempt. Although our intuitiveness is expressed in different forms– having a gut feeling, having a sixth sense, being suddenly aware, or just having a feeling about something– this is experienced by both sinners and saints. People often react to these intuitive impressions with statements like, "Oh I guess that was just me," or "I wonder where that thought came from." Usually they dismiss this gut feeling, not knowing that it is often an accurate impression of things that are unknowable to them at the time. Others believe that our intuition is relegated to the realm of the flesh and the devil. They often warn believers of the dangers incurred when they dabble in this so-called forbidden power.

This is not to say, however, that all intuition is good. For instance, intuitive people such as psychics, New Agers, clairvoyants and fortune tellers operate in a realm of divination, not in a legitimate realm of the Holy Spirit.

IMPRESSIONS

Receiving impressions, as we mentioned earlier, is nothing more than contemporary Christian slang. The phrase "I have an impression" as it is currently used by Christians is neither found in Scripture nor in the English dictionary. Therefore, under such circumstances it would be more appropriate to say, "the Lord has made me aware" or "I perceive by the Spirit of God."

Sources of Receiving Prophetic Revelation

And immediately when Jesus perceived in his spirit that they so reasoned within themselves, he said unto them, Why reason ye these things in your hearts?

Mark 2:8

But Jesus perceived their wickedness, and said, Why tempt ye me, ye hypocrites?

Matthew 22:18

For I perceive that thou art in the gall of bitterness, and in the bond of iniquity.

Acts 8:23

And said unto them, Sirs, I perceive that this voyage will be with hurt and much damage, not only of the lading and ship, but also of our lives.

Acts 27:10

Unlike the word impression, the word perceived is used several places in the New Testament. In Mark 2:8, Jesus "perceived in his Spirit" the thoughts of the scribes. In Matthew 22:18, when dealing with the disciples of the pharisees, He perceived their wickedness and also when Peter was addressing Simon the sorcerer he said "I perceive that thou art in the gall of bitterness" (Acts 8:23). Also, Paul while sailing on a ship from Alexandria said to those on board with him, "Sirs, I perceive that this voyage will be with hurt and much damage" (Acts 27:10).

This concept of prophetic perception is a common occurrence in the lives of most prophetic people today. Some of the most accurate information received and released by most prophetic people comes as a result of this principle. You can call it "sanctified gut feelings" or "spirit awareness," but the bottom line is this: God has heightened our awareness to things around us. By virtue of this dynamic, we need to develop a sensitivity to the inner nudging of the Holy Spirit. This will enable you to perceive things such as imminent danger, hidden illness, secret sins and the thoughts and intents of people's hearts.

The next way of receiving prophetic revelation is through developing our recreated human spirit.

Love not the world, neither the things that are in the world. If any man love the world, the love of the Father is not in him.

For all that is in the world, the lust of the flesh, and the lust of the eyes, and the pride of life, is not of the Father, but is

of the world.

And the world passeth away, and the lust thereof: but he that doeth the will of God abideth for ever.

But ye have an unction from the Holy One, and ye know all things.

I have not written unto you because ye know not the truth, but because ye know it, and that no lie is of the truth.

Let that therefore abide in you, which ye have heard from the beginning. If that which ye have heard from the beginning shall remain in you, ye also shall continue in the Son, and in the Father.

And this is the promise that he hath promised us, even eternal life.

These things have I written unto you concerning them that seduce you.

But the anointing which ye have received of him abideth in you, and ye need not that any man teach you: but as the same anointing teacheth you of all things, and is truth, and is no lie, and even as it hath taught you, ye shall abide in him.

> I John 2:15-17, 20-21, 24-27

Prophetic Development

In studying the epistle of John, we find he was a man that was very concerned about spiritual development. John was interested in bringing the Body of Christ to spiritual maturity. He writes to children and to adults. This is a man to whom God has revealed a chartered plan to spiritual maturity. He possessed a blueprint for corporate understanding and growth in the Kingdom of God.

The most significant thing that the apostle John did was to bring the believer, the New Covenant men and women, into contact with the Holy Spirit. As a New Covenant believer, the issue is not whether God is speaking. The Scripture implicitly declares that God desires to speak to us. But the issue is over the methods of communication that God uses. How does God communicate? God wants to interact with us on a daily basis through the Holy Spirit. And He desires to lead us and to instruct us and there is not one simple area of our lives in which He is not interested. But the real issue is, how does God speak to us? How can I come in contact with Him and learn to hear and discern and to understand His Voice on a daily basis? As long as the devil can blind our eyes to that aspect of relationship or to the methods of communication that God uses, then he has us exactly where he wants us, because we will never clearly hear what the Holy Spirit is saying.

Sources of Receiving Prophetic Revelation

If Jesus said, "My sheep know My Voice," and if John said, "You have an anointing from the Holy One and know all things and that same anointing which abides within you produces the ability to teach you," then evidently there is an access vehicle of communication that God wants to use. Evidently, there is a sure way to identify the Voice of God when He is speaking to you. Christians often ask, "When I listen to God, how do I know that it is God? How do I know that it is not a false spirit or a familiar voice or a satanic influence?" Or, "When I listen to God, how do I know that I'm not hearing my own feelings? When God speaks to me, how do I know which voice is the right voice because I often hear two voices?"

Identifying the Voice of God is very essential to having confidence in what God is saying and doing. In order to have confidence in what is being said, you must first of all be able to identify the voice of the one that is talking. With knowledge comes confidence. With understanding comes the ability to lock your faith in and to follow thereafter. Until you understand the Guide, you will never understand the directions in which He is leading you. Consequently, your life is going to be filled with a series of questions like, "Why this?" and "Why that?"

It is important that we know that truth is not independent of thought. Truth is not a feeling. It is not a theory. It is not an attitude and it is not a perception. Truth is not a variable. Truth is a constant. Opinions are variable and perceptions are variable. Truth is a constant. Truth is unwavering and Truth is a Person. Everything that God says must be in harmony and in conjunction with His Word and must not contradict His thought.

The reason why God gave us the written Scripture and the reason why God speaks beyond the Scripture, is because you will encounter situations in your life that are not covered by Scriptures. If you seek to please God and to honor Him and be found faithful with that which God has given you, you will find yourself at a point presented with situations and circumstances in which the Word of God does not give a clear definition. For example, the Bible does not tell you where to live, whether in Africa, in Asia, in Russia or in Mexico. The Word of God does not give explicit instructions for each one of us to let us know our assigned geographical location.

But the Holy Spirit has something to say about where you should live. He desires to lead you into the green pastures that have been allotted for you. The Word of God also did not say whether you should marry Peter, Paul or Michael.

Sources of Receiving Prophetic Revelation

The Word of God did not indicate the name of the person you should marry. Yet, the Holy Spirit desires to be intricately involved in bringing you together with your mate for life. The Word of God did not specifically tell you how many children you should bear. If you have the strength, the support and finances to have one, three or twenty, that is your responsibility. Yet, the Holy Spirit wants to be involved in the bringing forth of your family and show you how big your family should be. So these are ways in which the Scriptures are limited in their ability to bring specific guidance to our lives. But, the Holy Spirit is available to lead you, to guide you and to instruct you in every area of endeavor and decision.

The Bible did not say whether a Lexus is better than a Mercedes Benz or if a Volvo is better than a Cadillac, but the Holy Spirit is available to lead you into making the right choice for you. God wants to speak to you on a daily basis. While the Word of God is not clear in all of these areas, there are certain principles which support that these decisions are eternal. If you can learn these principles, then you can learn the attitudes of God, the heart of God and how He feels about certain situations.

And I will pray the Father, and he shall give you another Comforter, that he may abide with you for ever;

John 14:16

Jesus called the Holy Spirit "another Comforter. " Jesus was the first Comforter. The Holy Spirit was the second Comforter. He is One that is called alongside to help. One who will complete the initiative of the first Comforter. As a Comforter, called alongside to help, He will lead us and guide us. Now, let's look and examine some of the ways God speaks to us.

OUR RECREATED HUMAN SPIRIT

At times, many of God's people find it difficult to hear the Voice of God through their recreated human spirit. This is important, because God is still speaking to His people today through their recreated human spirit. Our recreated human spirit has two guides: the inward witness and the inward voice. The inward witness is different from the inward voice.

The inward witness is something inside of you that produces a check, a red light instructing you to stop. It is not a voice. It is an inward intuition. It is an inward knowing. It

Sources of Receiving Prophetic Revelation

is a feeling that is produced in our spirit and not in our mind or body. If the Body of Christ learns and continues to follow the leadings that are produced from our inward witness, the Church will see and receive great guidance in every area of life. We would be able to avoid certain pitfalls that the enemy has placed in our path. The inward witness produces a burden for a thing. The word "burden" actually means "creating a sense of responsibility."

For thou wilt save the afflicted people; but wilt bring down high looks.

For thou wilt light my candle: the LORD my God will enlighten my darkness.

Psalms 18:27-28

Here, God lights our lamp. The Bible says that "The spirit of man is the candle of the Lord...." That means that our spirit is a lamp. It is a light. It guides and directs us. What then happens in the leading from the inward witness, is that God lights our spirit (which is the lamp), and allows us to see all of the tricks, schemes and devices of the enemy that lurk in the darkness. God allows us to avoid pitfalls by lighting our lamps. When the light goes on in us, we immediately have this knowing– this intuition– and are able to see the right path and make the right decisions.

The problem is, many of us do not follow the inward witness. We go in our own directions and make our own decisions. The inward witness demands faith, trust and complete reliance upon the leading of God. Many say to themselves, "What if God is not actually leading me?" The problem is that the spirit man has not been properly trained. We must respond to the inward witness by faith, knowing that God is actually speaking and leading.

> **But as it is written, Eye hath not seen, nor ear heard, neither have entered into the heart of man, the things which God hath prepared for them that love him.**
>
> **But God hath revealed them unto us by his Spirit: for the Spirit searcheth all things, yea, the deep things of God.**
>
> **For what man knoweth the things of a man, save the spirit of man which is in him? even so the things of God knoweth no man, but the Spirit of God.**
>
> **But the natural man receiveth not the things of the Spirit of God: for they are foolishness unto him: neither can he know them, because they are spiritually discerned.**

Sources of Receiving Prophetic Revelation

But he that is spiritual judgeth all things, yet he himself is judged of no man.

I Corinthians 2:9-11,14-15

The Spirit itself beareth witness with our spirit, that we are the children of God:

Romans 8:16

The spirit of man is the candle of the LORD, searching all the inward parts of the belly.

Proverbs 20:27

The Holy Spirit desires to invade us. Let me put it this way: He wants to light our lamps. You may have a dead candle. You may be dead in your trespasses and dead in your sins, but the Holy Spirit Himself will come and bear witness to your spirit that you are a child of God through the new birth process. He will strike the match and light your lamp. He will bring spiritual enlightenment because He sets up residence within you, as His headquarters, within your spirit man. The Holy Spirit headquarters in our spirit. Our spirit becomes His communication center. He then begins to communicate to us by speaking to our spirit through the inward witness– words, thoughts, feelings– that you know are not of yourself, but they are somehow within you.

Prophetic Development

The Holy Spirit will communicate through feelings. That is part of perceiving in the Spirit. This is why, when you have done certain things, you may feel a great feeling within your spirit man of peace and joy. You find that the Holy Spirit is pleased and He is communicating peace and joy. There are other times when things are wrong and the Holy Spirit is displeased and He communicates within you a grieving or a sorrow. The Holy Spirit can warn you by communicating with you through a tightness in your gut. Now, we are not talking about natural feelings. The Holy Spirit can communicate to you through promptings, leadings, and perceivings that may not be outright words, but they are inner knowings.

And when Simon saw that through laying on of the apostles' hands the Holy Ghost was given, he offered them money,

Saying, Give me also this power, that on whomsoever I lay hands, he may receive the Holy Ghost.

But Peter said unto him, Thy money perish with thee, because thou hast thought that the gift of God may be purchased with money.

Thou hast neither part nor lot in this matter: for thy heart is not right in the sight of God.

Sources of Receiving Prophetic Revelation

Repent therefore of this thy wickedness, and pray God, if perhaps the thought of thine heart may be forgiven thee.

For I perceive that thou art in the gall of bitterness, and in the bond of iniquity.

Acts 8:18-23

There are times that you just know. How? Through spiritual perception. The spirit of a man goes out before the man. That is why people with the same spirit will usually find each other. People that have homosexual spirits have a very powerful demonic way of finding one another. That is the counterfeit to the genuine knowing of people by the spirit. That is why immorality will join with one another. That is why there is usually more unity in rebellion than there is in righteousness. Although it should not be this way, it usually is. Those in rebellion usually can attract to themselves others with the same rebellious spirit. From the above Scripture, you find that Paul was able to perceive that Simon was in the gall of bitterness.

THE INWARD VOICE

The inward voice is the voice of the conscience. It is the voice that echoes out of our conscience. Everybody has a conscience, whether a believer or an unbeliever. It is like a buzzer that sounds inside of us. With our conscience, we can tell if God is leading and speaking to us or not. When God begins to speak to you and you disobey Him, you can feel your conscience hurting. A lot of us might wonder if our conscience can actually be dependable. Our conscience can always be dependable, if our spirit man has become new.

I say the truth in Christ, I lie not, my conscience also bearing me witness in the Holy Ghost,

Romans 9:1

Look at what Paul was saying in Romans 9:1. He said he was not lying, and the reason he knew this was because his conscience was being enlightened and prompted by the Holy Spirit.

And Paul, earnestly beholding the council, said, Men and brethren, I have lived in all good conscience before God until this day.

Acts 23:1

In Acts 23:1, Paul began to tell the Sanhedrin that he has lived and walked before God performing all of his duty with

Sources of Receiving Prophetic Revelation

a good conscience. Why? Because his conscience was constantly being enlightened and prompted by the Holy Spirit.

The steps of a good man are ordered by the LORD: and he delighteth in his way.

Psalms 37:23

What does this word "order" mean? If I am going to be ordered by the Lord in my directive of going out and coming in, then what does it mean to be "ordered?" Here we see David using the Hebrew word, which means "to be erect" or "to stand perpendicular."

What this therefore means is that the steps of a good man are erected or standing perpendicular by the Lord. The Hebrew word also contains another element of thought. It means to be directed, established, and led. It implies more than just direction. It includes divine appointment, prosperity and everything that pertains to the covenant promise of God. All this is contained in the word "order." Therefore we can say that the steps of a good man are established, directed, prospered, blessed, divinely appointed, and are established with strength and ability to stand perpendicular. It is all contained in being led by the Spirit. Being led by the Spirit is being established in the will of God. It is being directed by the Spirit of God and prospering in the Word of God. This must become a lifestyle to us.

If ye be willing and obedient, ye shall eat the good of the land:

Isaiah 1:19

Hearing the Voice of God is not what we do in a crisis. But it is a complete lifestyle that is sanctioned by obedience. When I obey God's Word for my life, I am opening the door for a consistent flow of communication with my Father. If you have a problem hearing the Voice of God, the first question you must ask yourself is whether or not you are obeying what the Word of God says to do. Are you doing what God has set forth clearly in the Word of God for you to do? If you are not good in obeying the Word of God, you will never be sensitive in hearing the Voice of God. It is a lifestyle of obedience.

Being led of the Holy Spirit often involves the introduction of God's ordained circumstances into our lives. Often, God will introduce circumstances into our lives to gain our attention. There are circumstances that are of God and there are circumstances that are not of God. If we don't know how to differentiate between what is of God and what is not of God, we will find ourselves following the wrong thing.

> **Woe unto them that call evil good, and good evil; that put darkness for light, and light for darkness; that put bitter for sweet, and sweet for bitter!**
>
> **Isaiah 5:20**

There is a definite, distinguishable line between God-ordained circumstances for our growth and development, and the circumstances that the devil introduces into our lives to sidetrack us. Circumstances alone cannot be taken as a reliable guide for the will of God in your life.

However, circumstances will be introduced, and they must be supported by two things. First, what does the Word of God have to say about these circumstances? God introduces circumstances in our lives for refinement, but these circumstances never contradict His established Word. Second, the measuring stick must be the witness of the Holy Spirit.

Prophetic Development

You see, we have a strange charismatic philosophy that temptations, testings and trials are only introduced when we miss God or when we sin. And when the enemy begins to challenge and buffet us, the first thing that we always do is ask God if there is any sin in our lives. Even though this is right, we must not camp there. We must be ready to move further. But a great deal of us are wrestling because we think that we have missed God or have sinned. We literally think that we are the elite crowd and that we are not susceptible to the contrary winds that must blow into each of our lives. There is no favoritism in the Kingdom of God, and God is not a respecter of persons.

When you find yourself in temptation and trials, you must know that they have come for your spiritual refinement.

Behold, I will send my messenger, and he shall prepare the way before me: and the Lord, whom ye seek, shall suddenly come to his temple, even the messenger of the covenant, whom ye delight in: behold, he shall come, saith the LORD of hosts.

But who may abide the day of his coming? and who shall stand when he appeareth? for he is like a refiner's fire, and like fullers' soap:

Malachi 3:1-2

Sources of Receiving Prophetic Revelation

God is forever sitting as a Refiner. He is going to begin with the sons of Levi, because judgment first begins with the House of the Lord. It is going to begin with the priesthood. We sit around looking at ministers and watch them fall. We see them being purged and judged and we get the wrong idea that their circumstance is the location of the heat. That is partly true. The heat is going to come upon all of the Body of Christ generally, before God begins to wrap up His Church. And where we have sat criticizing, mocking and scorning in self-righteous attitudes, God is going to come upon every believer and He is going to purge us of our judgmentalism, our critical spirits, our mockery and the shameful lack of discipline that stains our tongues. It begins with the sons of Levi. But it will continue to the other members in the Body. The process of refinement is never easy, but it is vital to your spiritual development.

THE CONFIRMATION OF WITNESSES

God was very faithful to Old Testament Israel with a cloud in the day and a pillar of fire by night. He was meticulous in how He protected them and how He guided them. Today, there are unnecessary hurts, loss of revenues, broken relationships, terrible mistakes and tragedies in life because people simply do not know how God directs. People who often trust only one way of guidance usually want their own way. They know that if they go and get counsel, or if they go and examine that direction with the other ways God directs, they know that the answer will be no. So they say, I am trusting those three phone call confirmations. They end up losing.

This is the third time I am coming to you. In the mouth of two or three witnesses shall every word be established.

II Corinthians 13:1

Here is the key to God's navigation system. God is saying here that He will not allow us to be led by just one principle. There is too much danger. I am not saying at any time one is not right, but I am saying that, to make a major decision in your life, God will not allow you to be led by just one. The rule is, two or three at a minimum.

After they were come to Mysia, they assayed to go into Bithynia: but the Spirit suffered them not.

Acts 16:7

Sources of Receiving Prophetic Revelation

Then the Spirit said unto Philip, Go near, and join thyself to this chariot.

Acts 8:29

Several years ago, the cargo door of a Boeing 707 from Hawaii blew out and caused structural damage up above to the seating section. A number of the passengers were blown out into the Pacific Ocean and were killed. What was not in the news was that there was a Spirit-filled Christian who was sitting right next to where the accident occurred who gave a testimony and said that just moments before the disaster, he heard a Voice in his spirit saying he should move to another area of the plane. He hesitated a moment and the Voice said move now. He did not hear it audibly. He heard it in his spirit. So he got up and moved to an unoccupied seat in the coach area and moments later the section where he had been sitting was ripped out. Now that is the ability to be led by an inner conviction, the small Voice of the Holy Spirit which gives you a thought, a picture or an impression inside. This is exactly what Paul experienced. He and the men were on their way to their intended assignment. But they were stopped by the Spirit. They were stopped by this inner conviction or this impression that we are talking about and redirected by a vision to a different assignment. The key thing here is that Paul understood the leading of the Spirit. The people with him trusted his ability to hear the Voice of God, and also his ability to respond to that leading, no matter what form of leading the Lord chose.

THE ABIDING STRENGTH OF THE ANOINTING

Little children, it is the last time: and as ye have heard that antichrist shall come, even now are there many antichrists; whereby we know that it is the last time.

They went out from us, but they were not of us; for if they had been of us, they would no doubt have continued with us: but they went out, that they might be made manifest that they were not all of us.
But ye have an unction from the Holy One, and ye know all things.

I have not written unto you because ye know not the truth, but because ye know it, and that no lie is of the truth.

I John 2:18-21

Anyone who is messing up their life, is messing it up on purpose. What John is trying to say to us here is that the anointing of the Holy Spirit, the anointing that Christ has anointed you with, is on the inside. Even without the baptism of the Holy Spirit externally on you, around you and over you, when you got saved, the Holy Spirit came inside of you to abide and to seal you to the day of redemption and you received an anointing inside of you. At that moment, you have the capability to know all things by the anointing. It gives the capacity for truth, not from an external source, so that you don't always have to have everything from the outside. When John says "you know all things," most of us would say we don't know all things. Now there will always be a couple of people who will say they know all things, but most of us know that in the natural we don't know all things. However, John is saying that by the anointing, the potential and capability for everything you need in the realm of knowledge is available to the believer inside, by the anointing of Christ. So when John said that you need no man to teach you, he is not saying that we know everything and don't need to come to church services or fellowship with the believers. What he means is that the anointing inside will teach you when you hear the truth from God's Word and it will bear witness with the Spirit of truth inside of you. He will reveal and produce clarity to what is being taught so that you receive insight. It is the anointing inside of you that produces the insight and helps you to receive and believe in what you have read and listened to as coming from God. A good example of this is the example of mothers with children. Mothers really don't have to go to a four-year college to know how to interpret the cry of their children. They can easily interpret the cry to mean time to eat, time to sleep or even time for attention. In all of these interpretations, they are usually ninety percent to a hundred percent right. If you ask the mothers how they know the interpretation of the cry, they will tell you that they don't know how, they just know from inside what it means. They have that anointing or unction inside of them, so they don't need anyone to teach them. They got it intuitively.

The anointing of the Spirit in you will communicate through your flesh, bearing witness to the Holy Spirit that is in you. That is why when you hear something taught that is Biblical and right, you say "Amen" because it is the Spirit in you that is revealing that, even if you have never thought about it. The anointing in you knows all things, but it does not mean that you know all things. It just means that with the Holy Spirit in you, you have the capacity in you at any moment to know anything that is knowable.

PITFALLS OF THE INWARD LEADING

The problem with this kind of leading is that it is the most mystical and the most subjective of all of the various ways God leads and directs. It is totally based on what you feel, what you sense, what you see and what you hear in your own spirit. When people say, "The Lord told me that we are to go there," by what you have just said or done, you have taken the leadership, or the Holy Spirit-inspired counselor, out of the process of counseling with you, because you have already appealed to the highest authority. This is the most dangerous form of leading because it is subjective, mystical and it is just what you feel. It does not give any boundaries to Scripture, to Godly counsel or any of the other ways God speaks. Anybody who always wants to do what they want to, will always tell you God has spoken to them to go there or to do that thing. Is it that God does not speak or cannot speak? The answer is, God is still speaking and will continue to speak to you and me. But we must be aware and watchful of the pitfalls in this way of leading because of the subjectivity and mysticism of this form of leading. That is why it is very important to check it with the other ways God leads for more clarity and insight.

Often the reason why most believers don't go to leadership or consult the other ways God speaks for more clarity, is that they are afraid that they will hear "No." If you are afraid that someone in leadership or one of the other forms of leading will produce red lights or say "No," then just admit to yourself that you really don't want to do the will of God. You just want to do what you want to do, because if you really want to do the will of God, the word "No" will never scare you. Anything as subjective as the inner leading of the Holy Spirit has to be properly balanced. When we study the context of I John 2, we will see the danger that is inherent in just following the Spirit subjectively. Jesus was able to follow the Spirit perfectly. He said I only do what I see my Father do. What was He talking about? He was not seeing the Father physically. He was seeing Him from inside His heart. He instinctively knew within how to react and what to do in every situation.

THE DANGER OF LIVING SUBJECTIVELY AND MYSTICALLY

Love not the world, neither the things that are in the world. If any man love the world, the love of the Father is not in him.

Sources of Receiving Prophetic Revelation

And all they that heard it wondered at those things which were told them by the shepherds.

I John 2:15, 18

There are a lot of believers who live subjectively and mystically. If they see seven cars lined up in a row and they love the seventh one, they immediately conclude that is the car they should buy, because the number seven is God's number of perfection, or because they had a dream last night. Even though the dream is not a bad dream, you cannot be led by your dream ALONE. You must subject it to the other ways God speaks to produce accuracy and direction. There are a few more guide posts to line up before running off the cliff with a word from a dream. All the guide posts must be lined up.

Look at the Scripture that we just read. Why did John start by warning us not to love the world? When you are in love with God, walking with Him and abiding in Him, you instinctively know what to do. John is warning us that we are in a subjective area when operating in this form of leading. It can easily be confused with other things that come up inside, just like the spirits that are not of the Spirit. Why can't inner conviction be the place we stop? Because of the mixtures in us that can pollute and come up the same way as the Spirit of God. If our appetites were completely holy, pure and sanctified, we would be safe. But John went on to say in verse 18 that there is another anointing. It is not the Christ anointing. It is the antichrist anointing. Antichrist does not mean "against" Christ. It means "instead of" or "in place of." How do you identify this anointing? John said there are some things that you have to watch for, so that you don't get a false anointing. There are the antichrist spirits and these spirits are the lust of the flesh, the lust of the eyes and the pride of life. The lust of the flesh speaks of pleasure. It is to feel something. The lust of the eyes is the desire for possessions, to have something. The pride of life wants position, to be someone. These three can counterfeit the real anointing.

THE ANTICHRIST ANOINTING

Now there are three dimensions to self-gratification: to feel something, to have something and to be something. The devil has no new plans. He uses all of them against us. John says, "Watch out. Don't love these things. These loves and these affections can feel just like the leadings of God, because they are from within. That is an antichrist leading."

Sources of Receiving Prophetic Revelation

And the serpent said unto the woman, Ye shall not surely die:

For God doth know that in the day ye eat thereof, then your eyes shall be opened, and ye shall be as gods, knowing good and evil.

And when the woman saw that the tree *was* good for food, and that it *was* pleasant to the eyes, and a tree to be desired to make *one* wise, she took of the fruit thereof, and did eat, and gave also unto her husband with her; and he did eat.

Genesis 3:4-6

Let us look at a couple of examples. In the above Scripture, God instructed Adam not to eat of the fruit of the tree of the knowledge of good and evil. But the woman saw that the tree was good for food (pleasure) and she saw that it was a tree to be desired to make one wise and so it would be good to possess that possession. Then the serpent said that if you eat of it, you shall be as God; that is, be somebody (position). Right here are the three weapons in the satanic arsenal. There are no new tricks. They are always the same because they work. God is not against pleasure. He is not against possessions. He is not against position. If you humble yourself, God will exalt you. He is talking about illegitimate desires, illegitimate appetites that are in our flesh, and they feel just like the leading of the Holy Spirit.

> **And the men of Israel said, Have ye seen this man that is come up? surely to defy Israel is he come up: and it shall be, that the man who killeth him, the king will enrich him with great riches, and will give him his daughter, and make his father's house free in Israel.**
>
> **I Samuel 17:25**

In this Scripture, you find three things that King Saul promised or offered to the man who would go and fight against Goliath. The first thing he promised was his daughter in marriage, and this is symbolic of the desire for PLEASURE. Second, he promised to give the person who killed Goliath land to possess. He would make him a landowner. This is symbolic of the desire for POSSESSIONS. Finally, he promised to let the person who killed Goliath live tax-free. That is, the person's new position in Israel would be a tax-free POSITION. These are counterfeit motives to get somebody to fight the giant. Motives are what drive all of us. We need to be driven and motivated by the Holy Spirit. We need to know that whatever we are doing is motivated by and for the Holy Spirit and not by our flesh or our unmet needs. God uses motives and the devil uses motives. They both come from the inside, which makes it such a subtle deception. We

Sources of Receiving Prophetic Revelation

must always make sure that we are led by the Spirit. However, there is another kind of leading and another kind of motive. It is counterfeit and it is rooted in these three desires.

And Jesus, when he was baptized, went up straightway out of the water: and, lo, the heavens were opened unto him, and he saw the Spirit of God descending like a dove, and lighting upon him:

Matthew 3:16

Then was Jesus led up of the Spirit into the wilderness to be tempted of the devil.

And when he had fasted forty days and forty nights, he was afterward an hungred.

And when the tempter came to him, he said, If thou be the Son of God, command that these stones be made bread.

But he answered and said, It is written, Man shall not live by bread alone, but by every word that proceedeth out of the mouth of God.

Then the devil taketh him up into the holy city, and setteth him on a pinnacle of the temple,

And saith unto him, If thou be the Son of God, cast thyself down: for it is written, He shall give his angels charge

concerning thee: and in their hands they shall bear thee up, lest at any time thou dash thy foot against a stone.

Jesus said unto him, It is written again, Thou shalt not tempt the Lord thy God.

Again, the devil taketh him up into an exceeding high mountain, and sheweth him all the kingdoms of the world, and the glory of them;

And saith unto him, All these things will I give thee, if thou wilt fall down and worship me.

Then saith Jesus unto him, Get thee hence, Satan: for it is written, Thou shalt worship the Lord thy God, and him only shalt thou serve.

Matthew 4:1-10

This is another example. Jesus was baptized by John at the river Jordan and then was baptized in the Holy Spirit by the evidence of a dove coming upon Him. Afterward, He was driven by the Holy Spirit into the wilderness. While in the wilderness, satan offered Jesus three things. The first thing he offered Jesus was to turn the stones into bread. This temptation tripped up the first Adam and caused him to eat the fruit, but it did not trip up the last Adam, Jesus. Jesus had no

Sources of Receiving Prophetic Revelation

release in His spirit (in His inner guidance system) and so He said that man shall not live by bread alone, but by every word that proceedeth out of the mouth of God. He knew it was a set-up and He said no.

Second, the devil offered or promised Jesus all of the kingdoms and his glory for a possession. The subtle bait here is not just the possession, but the glory that comes out of the possession. Finally, the devil told Him to jump off the temple and that God would give His angels charge over Him. What he was actually saying was that he wanted Jesus to prove His position by jumping. Jesus refused because He knew His position and did not need to prove it. If you look at a fallen minister or a fallen believer, you will find these three things in their lives. Every one of them ran through red lights before they smashed up. We need to increase and improve our discernment so that a lot more people can arrive safely at their destination.

THE THREE GODS OF ISRAEL

In the nation of Israel, there were three false gods that plagued them throughout the entire Old Testament. They were Ashteroth, Baal and Molech. Ashteroth was the goddess of sex and pleasure. Baal was the goddess of increase (financial increase). People in the Old Testament understood then that there were ruling spirits over certain areas. A non-covenant Israelite would sneak out on his back property and build himself a little rock altar so that the high priests wouldn't see it. If they did, he would be stoned to death. He would make sacrifices to these spirits to appease and get the favor of Baal, so that she would bless his crops and he would prosper. But God hated the idolatry because they were looking to Baal for financial increase, instead of looking to God. Many Christians still do the same thing today.

Molech was the idol that had a furnace in its belly. People would offer their babies for the promise of promotion and elevation in the community. The root of Molech is the pride of life. Molech is the god of abortion. "I cannot have a baby because it is going to ruin my career. It is going to cramp my life."

The potential is unlimited to be led by the Holy Spirit. There is potential in every believer to know all truth and to be led by inner conviction, but the guard rails have to do with the watching out for the appetite. God can only lead you by holy, sanctified, pure desire and appetite. He will even use your desires to pull you into purpose and destiny. If you are abiding in Christ and delighting in the Lord, every desire you have in that position is going to be pure. The inner conviction always works when we are abiding in God. The problem is that sometimes we are in and sometimes we are out.

GOD SPEAKS THROUGH HIS WORD

God also speaks through His Word or through Scriptures. A lot of believers fail to really depend on God's ability to speak to them through His Word. They prefer a more "sophisticated" way. When God speaks to you through His Word, it is the same as a ministry gift coming to you and saying, "Thus saith the Lord." The degree of value that you place on the Voice of God released through His Word will produce the degree of change His Word will determine concerning what the Word is directed to do. I have noticed many times that when God speaks to us through His Word, that particular scripture or message from the Word tightly grabs hold of your spirit. Your spirit man leaps– just as the baby in Elisabeth's womb leaped when she came in contact with Mary. Your soul echoes a sound like that of a trumpet. You know for sure that God is speaking to you. In other words, that Scripture becomes personified and immediately connects to your spirit. Out of the *logos* leaps a *rhema* word sent directly to meet your immediate need.

All scripture is given by inspiration of God, and is profitable for doctrine, for reproof, for correction, for instruction in righteousness:

II Timothy 3:16

The Bible says all Scripture is given by inspiration. The Greek word for INSPIRATION is "OPNEUSTOS." It is only recorded once in the New Testament. It literally means "God-breathed," with the prefix "THEOS" meaning "God" and "PEO" meaning "breath." That gives us the insight to see that God breathed His truth into the hearts and minds of the writers of the Scripture. The Word of God is God HIMSELF speaking to us. We must take the Word spoken to us by God through His Word very seriously. The Word is the life of God. So when He speaks He produces life in us, if we will move in obedience to His Word. We must pay great attention to this avenue or medium of God speaking. The Bible tells us the purpose of the Scripture being given: for doctrine, for reproof, for correction and for instruction. Let's just concentrate on two of these purposes: "correction" and "instruction." The word CORRECTION in the Greek is "EPANORTHOSIS." "ORTHOS" means "straight." The term suggests "restoration to an upright or a right state and improvement." Whenever God speaks to us through His

Word to correct us, God is actually restoring us to an upright or to a right state.

INSTRUCTION comes from the Greek word "PADDY" which comes from "PAIS." This word means "child," and is also derived from the verb "PAD," which in classical Greek means "to train children." So the literal meaning of "PADDY" is "child training." But Biblical writers felt and understood that all effectual instruction for the sinful children of men includes and implies chastening. Since instruction is thought of as mainly intellectual, training is a more adequate translation. When God speaks to us, we must discover the purpose for which the Word has been directed. Is it for doctrine, reproof, correction or instruction in righteousness? Once we find out the purpose, then we must yield and allow God to have His way. We must accept His Word and allow His Word to fulfill His purpose in us.

My son, keep thy father's commandment, and forsake not the law of thy mother:

Proverbs 6:20

Thy word *is* a lamp unto my feet, and a light unto my path.

Psalm 119:105

God has a way of guiding His children. We want to live successful lives. We want to finish this life well. God has divine principles that He uses to keep us on course and navigate our lives, so that we can actually finish our life without making any unfortunate mistakes. It is possible to live life without any major mistakes. It is not possible as a human being not to make slight or minor mistakes, but the key thing is that it will not be fatal or a major mistake that ruins and destroys your life, the life of your family or your ministry.

THE MARRIAGE OF THE WORD AND THE SPIRIT

God's Word is for guidance. The Spirit plays a part, but not without the Word. The Word plays a part, but also not without the Spirit. The Word and the Spirit must be married to produce accurate and effective guidance.

In the beginning God created the heaven and the earth.

And the earth was without form, and void; and darkness was upon the face of the deep. And the Spirit of God moved upon the face of the waters.

And God said, Let there be light: and there was light.
And God said, Let us make man in our image, after our likeness: and let them have dominion over the fish of the sea,

Sources of Receiving Prophetic Revelation

And God said, Let us make man in our image, after our likeness: and let them have dominion over the fish of the sea,

and over the fowl of the air, and over the cattle, and over all the earth, and over every creeping thing that creepeth upon the earth.

Genesis 1:1-3, 26

When God wants to invade the physical realm, He has a classic pattern for doing it that is repeated over and over in Scriptures. What you will see is that sometimes you don't have an exact word or a particular verse in Scripture concerning your guidance, but you have a pattern in Scripture or you have principles in Scriptures. It is an agreement of His Word and His Spirit that God always uses. He will never lead you by the Spirit and be in disagreement with His Word. He will never give you a Word that disagrees with His Spirit. They will always work in perfect harmony. Now, notice in the Scripture that the Holy Spirit is hovering or brooding over a created world that is without order. God's desire is to invade it. How is He going to do it? Notice verse three. It says God said, "Let there be light and there was light." See how the Spirit and the Word worked together to impact the natural or the physical realm? Then, in verse 26 the Bible says, "then

God said let us make man in our image, according to our likeness." In chapter 2, verse 7, we saw how God "formed man of the ground and breathed into his nostrils the breath of life and man became a living soul." What is the breath of life? The Spirit of God. When God was ready to make the world, the Spirit hovered over it. Then God spoke the Word and immediately order came out of confusion. Then He said, "Let us make man," that is His Word. And once man was made, God breathed into that man the Spirit of life and we have the creation of life.

When you are going to follow God, you must follow His Word and His Spirit. Make sure that these two are always in agreement. A lot of Christians spend their time in the Spirit. They emphasize the life in the Spirit. They can easily be deceived if they don't know the Word. For some reason, by the grace of God, they are very sensitive to the spiritual realm and sometimes they are right and sometimes they are wrong, but they don't know much Word. Then you have the other group of people that are much grounded in the Word and have no Spirit. Both extremes are wrong. Don't choose either of these. You want a balance of both in right harmony, if you follow the Scriptural pattern. All Word and no Spirit causes you to dry up. You become a pharisee, an adherent to the letter of the law that kills. You become mean, legalistic and

Sources of Receiving Prophetic Revelation

engender bondage without life. If you are all Spirit and no Word, you will become self-destructive and blow up. You will go nuts because you have no perimeters with which to bring order and you will have confusion. God is not the author of confusion, but of order. The combination of the Spirit and the Word will cause you to grow up. It is not one or the other. It is both in harmony to produce a mature Christian that has life and the right structure.

And the word of the LORD came unto me, saying,

Son of man, prophesy against the prophets of Israel that prophesy, and say thou unto them that prophesy out of their own hearts, Hear ye the word of the LORD;

Thus saith the Lord GOD; Woe unto the foolish prophets, that follow their own spirit, and have seen nothing!

Ezekiel 13:1-3

In this Scripture, God warns against the prophets who declare what they are saying to be from Him when actually it is not from Him. Then in verse 3, He says woe to the foolish prophets who follow their own spirit and have seen nothing. I am always afraid of immature Christians who are susceptible to the spirit realm. They don't know any Word, and someone who has a supernatural gift that is manifested through a familiar spirit can easily deceive them, because they don't know the Word. On the other hand, we don't want to be stuck on the Word without having any Spirit to give life and power and flow in the things of God. It is both of them. I have never met any Christian who doesn't lean more to one of these than the other. It does not mean that they are wrong, it is just their personal trait. It is how they were raised spiritually. It can always be adjusted and corrected to allow the flow of both. The adjustment and correction only happens when we are willing to respond to the spirit of change.

There is a principle in the Scripture where Jesus used wine and wineskins to illustrate the picture of the correspondence of the Word and the Holy Spirit to give us guidance. The Word corresponds to the wineskin. A wineskin holds the wine. It does not produce it. It just holds it. The new wine corresponds to the Holy Spirit. The wine (Holy Spirit) is alive. It is free flowing and powerful. To find its true expression, it cannot be left by itself. It has to come into a structure where it still has life, vitality, movement and power. The wineskin is the Word and the wine is the Holy Spirit. It is like a fountain pen. If I want to send a letter to my wife, I don't just get a piece of paper and a bottle of ink and just pour the ink on the writing paper and send it to her. She won't be

Sources of Receiving Prophetic Revelation

able to read it. It is definitely ink and writing paper, but she still can't read it. If I put the ink (the wine, the Holy Spirit) in the pen (the structure, the Word) and it channels the expression of the Holy Spirit so that it does not limit its ability to form words and letters, then I can effectively communicate with her. Now it is doing its job. On the other hand, if the structure is so tight that the ink cannot come out, then I still cannot write. It is not one or the other. It is a balance. Sometimes in churches we just want the Spirit of God to flow and He is all over the place. Nobody can tell what He did because there was confusion everywhere and there was no order to that expression. The Holy Spirit is free, but He is still not without restraint. He has structure and He does not violate the Word. When the Holy Spirit operates within the structure of the Word, there is a release of direction, focus and impartation. The Spirit will get the job done. He flows through the structure of the Word. In the structure of the restriction of the Word, it gives us a limit, protection and balance. It is not to hinder you. It is to protect you.

THE WORD MADE LIFE

In the beginning was the Word, and the Word was with God, and the Word was God.

Prophetic Development

The same was in the beginning with God.

And the Word was made flesh, and dwelt among us, (and we beheld his glory, the glory as of the only begotten of the Father,) full of grace and truth.

John 1:1-2, 14

Here we have the Word made alive in Jesus Christ. Did the Word by Himself do any miracle for thirty years? No. The Word by Himself did not do any ministry for thirty years. Why not? Ministry cannot be accomplished without the Spirit. How did God invade the natural realm with Jesus? First, He came with the Word to a woman, a virgin named Mary. He told Mary that she was going to conceive and that the Holy Child she was going to bring forth was going to be the Son of God. Now Mary got the Word, but she said, "How can this be?" which means that getting the Word alone does not make it happen. An Angel said, "The Holy Spirit will overshadow you and conception will take place." Now, notice the pattern again. When God created the world, the Holy Spirit hovered over it, God spoke the Word and order came. Then when God made man, He spoke the Word and said let us make man in our own image. Then He breathed into that dead form the Spirit of God and we have created life. The same thing happened when God sent Jesus. The Word became flesh and dwelt among us. He did not do any miracle and any ministry until the Spirit of God at the baptism of John came upon Him. Then He launched His ministry from that moment forth. We got the Word guided by the Holy Spirit, and the Spirit energizing His Word. The anointing of the Word and the Spirit working in perfect harmony. Now, if you've got the Word in you and you've got the Spirit in you, you have the potential to walk like Jesus.

How God anointed Jesus of Nazareth with the Holy Ghost and with power: who went about doing good, and healing all that were oppressed of the devil; for God was with him.

Acts 10:38

How did this work in Jesus' ministry? The same way it is going to work in ours. The anointing of the Holy Spirit anointing the Word in us will cause the supernatural to be manifested. The guidance of the Spirit in Jesus' life was limited to the Father's will, nature, character and personality expressed in the written Word. Jesus never violated Scripture. He violated traditions and the pharisees' rule, but not the Word and the Holy Spirit. Whenever you come in agreement with the Word and the Holy Spirit concerning a situation, you always get a solution. People often say "I feel led" or "I feel the Holy Spirit told me to do this." And often they are calling a misdirection a leading. The problem is that they are going outside what the Father would do, and the reason they do this is because they don't know what the Father would do, because they do not know the Word. The more you read the Word, the more you see how Father does what He does. The Word reveals God, reveals His nature, His character, what He likes and what He does not like, and the Scripture becomes our wineskin. The Scripture then gives definition to the expression of the Holy Spirit. It gives us limitations, guidelines and liberty, as well.

GOD SPEAKING THROUGH DREAMS AND VISIONS

This is another area that has created much controversy among the Body of Christ. There are those who believe that God speaks through dreams and visions, and there are others who greatly criticize and despise dreams and visions as avenues through which God speaks. Those that despise dreams and visions believe that their era is gone and that these are the times that God only speaks through His Word and through our recreated human spirit.

It is quite true that God speaks through His Word and

through His Spirit. But it is also true that God still speaks through dreams and visions. It is unfathomable to say God does not speak through dreams and visions. I understand that dreams and visions have been greatly abused, but that does not mean we have to throw the baby out with the bathwater! We just need to understand God's ways!

The Church has not been properly taught about the operation, mechanism and interpretation of dreams and visions. It is a simple matter to have a dream or a vision. Yet it is another thing to understand what God is trying to convey to us and properly interpret it in the light and context of the Word. Every dream and vision must line up with the Word. Any dream and vision that does not line up with the Word of God is not worth considering.

But in order to understand and know whether a dream or a vision lines up with the Word or not, the believer must know how to interpret the symbolism of his dreams and visions. It is difficult for someone else to interpret your dream except that individual is prophetically led by the Spirit of God.

We must not depend totally on dreams and visions as the only way God speaks. If you don't have a dream or a vision, don't get upset. We must learn not to make a habit out of just wanting to have a dream or a vision. If it comes, it comes. It cannot be turned on. Dreams and visions must not be wrongly interpreted. If you don't understand your dreams or visions, ask your pastor or those who have been proven and gifted in the interpretations of dreams and visions.

Dreams and visions can come in various forms. Sometimes we get in very dangerous positions because we go to meetings and we hear men of God talk about what they have heard, how it came to them and then we try to lock the Spirit of God into a specific pattern or orbit. We hear popular ministers relate how God spoke to them, and a whole generation of ministers will try to go out by the arm of the flesh and create circumstances to duplicate what they've heard. Too many hear someone's testimony and think that God can only speak in that certain manner. Many of us end up fabricating fifty percent of what we say, and that is why we don't have results. The arm of flesh will never bring results. We must know that God can move through us uniquely. He does not have to move the same way with us as He moves with another person.

DREAMS

Sometimes in dreams things seen and heard are symbolic of the physical realm. The Old Testament is filled with vivid

Sources of Receiving Prophetic Revelation

dreams. It is filled with dreams that have changed the destiny of men, cities, nations, and entire groups of people. Dreams are contained in the prophetic revelations of God. You don't have to be a prophet or a prophetic minister. But as a prophetic generation, there is an access to dreams that the Spirit of God reveals unto us for understanding. In the Old Testament, God communicated twenty-two times in dreams to His people. Dreams are those things that God reveals in the night seasons for the purpose of information and establishment.

> **For God speaketh once, yea twice, yet man perceiveth it not.**
>
> **In a dream, in a vision of the night, when deep sleep falleth upon men, in slumberings upon the bed;**
>
> **Then he openeth the ears of men, and sealeth their instruction,**
>
> **That he may withdraw man from his purpose, and hide pride from man.**
>
> **Job 33:14-17**

Dreams usually come during the sleeping hour. In slumbering or in deep sleep, God says He will visit in the dream to seal up the instruction of men. In other words, God opens up their eyes and then seals up their instructions. One of the greatest mistakes you can make is to always go to someone to help interpret your dreams and visions. Whenever you have a dream, the first thing you should do is to take some time to seek God for the interpretation after judging whether it is from God or not. There is always grace, and there is always an anointing and understanding made available whenever the Spirit of God speaks.

If there is not an interpretation for the dream, don't waste your entire life seeking for an interpretation when there is none. Don't waste your time trying to determine something that may not have any measure of validity in the Kingdom of God. Seek God for the interpretation and if the interpretation does not come, go on with the rest of your life.

> **And he said, Hear now my words: If there be a prophet among you, I the LORD will make myself known unto him in a vision, and will speak unto him in a dream.**
>
> **Numbers 12:6**

The Lord has promised to speak to His people through visions and dreams. In the Old Testament, great references were constantly made to the prophets. Thank God, that today, God is not partial. God is still speaking through dreams and visions to His prophets. But He is also speaking to the other five-fold ministry gifts and the entire Body of Christ.

Since this is the time of restoration, God is also restoring confidence in Holy Ghost-inspired dreams and visions. We must not totally depend or rely solely upon them, but we must see them as a viable avenue of communication. We've been subjected to erroneous teachings in this area, which has made most Christians reject the Word of the Lord that came through a dream or vision. And some, who are particularly gifted in this area, have withdrawn and won't share what they're dreaming. They are afraid of being criticized by other believers.

In some churches and groups, it is almost an abomination to say that God spoke to you in a dream or in a vision. It is acceptable to say that God spoke through His Word or through our recreated human spirit. But it is like a crime to say to someone that God spoke to you in a dream.

Dreams have been taught to be very unreliable. Many have lost confidence in their own dreams and can't tell whether they are from God or not. As a result of this, many have placed dreams on the back burner. God will continue to speak through any channel or source that He desires. The Body of Christ must be flexible and ready to receive the accurate Word of the Lord through whatever means it comes.

There are ministers who strongly teach and believe that the reason Christians dream often is because of what they eat, see on TV, watch in the movies, or experience during the day. While it is true that there are dreams that are not inspired or given by God, it is also true that some are given by God. The problem is not with the dream, but the problem is with the individual being able to discern if it is from God or not. There is more than a one-hundred percent chance for a man or woman, whose spirit man is developed, sensitive and uprightly walking before God, to accurately pinpoint if a dream is God-inspired or satanically inspired. Just because an individual does not have a personal experience with dreams, this should not make him criticize or doubt the credence of their existence.

And he dreamed, and behold a ladder set up on the earth, and the top of it reached to heaven: and behold the angels of God ascending and descending on it.

And, behold, the LORD stood above it, and said, I am the LORD God of Abraham thy father, and the God of Isaac:

Sources of Receiving Prophetic Revelation

the land whereon thou liest, to thee will I give it, and to thy seed;

And thy seed shall be as the dust of the earth, and thou shalt spread abroad to the west, and to the east, and to the north, and to the south: and in thee and in thy seed shall all the families of the earth be blessed.

And, behold, I am with thee, and will keep thee in all places whither thou goest, and will bring thee again into this land; for I will not leave thee, until I have done that which I have spoken to thee of.

Genesis 28:12-15

This is a great example of God speaking to an individual through a dream. Jacob, in going to take for himself a wife, had a dream while resting in the city of Luz. The dream showed the illustration of a ladder hooking up to heaven and the angels of God ascending and descending on it. Thank God for the existence and reality of angels today!

Jacob had the option to either believe that it was from God or not. The Bible lets us know that when Jacob woke up from his sleep, he knew surely the Lord was in that place. Jacob knew he had an encounter with God. He knew that God was speaking to him in the dream. He did not discard the Word of the Lord. He received God's Word, even though it came through the avenue of a dream. As the Body of Christ begins to walk and operate in the spirit of accuracy and sharpness, the Church will begin to accurately discern, understand and interpret what God is saying through dreams and visions.

God is still speaking today through dreams, just as He is speaking through other avenues and channels. God, in this restorative movement of His Spirit, is visiting the Church through dreams and visions. It is not that God will not speak through any other source and avenue, but during this end time, the Church will see, experience and hear God through all of His available channels and sources.

> **And Joseph dreamed a dream, and he told it his brethren: and they hated him yet the more.**
>
> **And he said unto them, Hear, I pray you, this dream which I have dreamed:**
>
> **For, behold, we were binding sheaves in the field, and, lo, my sheaf arose, and also stood upright; and, behold, your sheaves stood round about, and made obeisance to my sheaf.**
>
> **And his brethren said to him, Shalt thou indeed reign over us? or shalt thou indeed have dominion over us? And they hated him yet the more for his dreams, and for his words.**

Sources of Receiving Prophetic Revelation

And he dreamed yet another dream, and told it his brethren, and said, Behold, I have dreamed a dream more; and, behold, the sun and the moon and the eleven stars made obeisance to me.

And he told it to his father, and to his brethren: and his father rebuked him, and said unto him, What is this dream that thou hast dreamed? Shall I and thy mother and thy brethren indeed come to bow down ourselves to thee to the earth?

Genesis 37:5-10

Joseph had two dreams in which his destiny was being unfolded right before His eyes. God can unfold your destiny and show you what is to come through a God-inspired dream. Even though he was just a young seventeen-year-old boy, God, through dreams, showed Joseph what was ahead. God literally showed him his future. As Joseph in his innocence began to share his dreams, his brethren became enraged with him. It is important that you don't share your dreams with just everyone. There are folks who will kill your dream. Dreams should be shared with people with whom you are divinely connected, and not with just every Tom, Dick and Harry.

Even though Joseph's father and brothers were upset concerning the dreams, they were able to discern, understand and interpret the meaning of the dream, although Joseph could not. The outcome of the dream was not manifested overnight, but in the process of time the dream was birthed from the spirit realm to the physical realm.

God will speak through any avenue or source He chooses. Most of the time, God will speak to an individual through an avenue that will be well understood and retained by that individual. Even though an individual may receive messages from his recreated human spirit and godly counsel, God, in cases of emergency and urgency, will speak to an individual through sources or channels with which they are familiar. He'll speak in a manner that they can easily discern, understand and fully interpret, until he or she is well developed in the other sources.

Most believers can easily detect when God is speaking to them because they've become skilled in one particular venue. Yet when God speaks through other manners, they find it much easier to disregard the message. They've become prejudiced and place God in a box, thinking that He'll only speak in one defined way. The Body of Christ in this generation, though they might have a specific avenue through

Sources of Receiving Prophetic Revelation

which the Spirit of God speaks to them, will experience the Word of the Lord through every available avenue because God is going to reveal Himself in many dimensions.

Now let's see what the New Testament had to say about dreams. There are some Christians who strongly believe that dreams and visions are for the Old Testament Church and not for the New Testament Church.

Then Joseph her husband, being a just man, and not willing to make her a public example, was minded to put her away privily.

But while he thought on these things, behold, the angel of the Lord appeared unto him in a dream, saying, Joseph, thou son of David, fear not to take unto thee Mary thy wife: for that which is conceived in her is of the Holy Ghost.
And she shall bring forth a son, and thou shalt call his name JESUS: for he shall save his people from their sins.
Then Joseph being raised from sleep did as the angel of the Lord had bidden him, and took unto him his wife:

Matthew 1:19-21,24

Joseph refused and would not believe the word from his wife Mary that was spoken to her by the Holy Spirit concerning her pregnancy and the birth of Jesus Christ. But he was able to believe and be persuaded by the angel of God who brought the Word of the Lord to him in a dream. Joseph had a God-inspired dream. Joseph could have said, "I don't believe in dreams." But that was not the case. The Bible says that he did everything the angel of the Lord bid him to do in the dream. That tells me that he was able to discern, understand and interpret the Word of the Lord from the dream. He obeyed the leading and the direction that he received through his dream.

> **And being warned of God in a dream that they should not return to Herod, they departed into their own country another way.**
>
> **Matthew 2:12**

In this case, the wise men were warned by God in a dream not to return to Herod. God spoke to the wise men concerning the plot, schemes and devices of King Herod toward the child Jesus in a dream. God instructed them not to return to Herod. This is an example of God speaking through dreams. The wise men believed God spoke to them. They did not ponder or doubt the message, but they discerned and understood that it was from God. They did not refuse the warning of God, even though it was through a dream. God is

Sources of Receiving Prophetic Revelation

doing the same thing today. God is still warning, instructing, directing and promoting His people through the God kind of dreams. Yet there are believers who will not adhere to their dreams because they have rendered such messages unacceptable. But whether you personally like it or not, God will continually speak to His Church through any channel He pleases.

> **Then Joseph her husband, being a just man, and not willing to make her a public example, was minded to put her away privily.**
>
> **But while he thought on these things, behold, the angel of the Lord appeared unto him in a dream, saying, Joseph, thou son of David, fear not to take unto thee Mary thy wife: for that which is conceived in her is of the Holy Ghost.**
>
> **Matthew 1:19,20**

Again, the angel of the Lord appeared to Joseph in a dream after the death of King Herod, bringing a Word of the Lord for a new direction. God instructed Joseph to leave Egypt and go to Israel because there were people who wanted to kill the baby Jesus. New directions can be received through dreams. God will do and is doing the same thing today. There have been men and women who have been warned of impending accidents, plots, schemes and devices of the enemy through dreams. Restoration has begun. God is restoring everything back to His original state and condition.

CAUSES OF DREAMS

A lot of things can cause us to have dreams. One of them may be our activities during the day. We are more likely to dream of whatever has dominated our minds or thoughts throughout that day. Such dreams are not birthed from God, but from our personal activity.

Another way we can have dreams is that dreams can come from the "memory bank" of our personal history. Many times, it is quite possible that good and bad experiences of our past and present may surface and show up while we are unguarded in our sleep. God may use these times to bring clarity and healing to these unresolved issues and problems. However it will not be proper to say that it came directly from God. It actually came from the "bank" of our personal hurts and tragedies.

Dreams can also come to us as a revelation of the enemy's plan against our lives, families, ministries and churches. Sometimes we have nightmares, horrifying dreams, disturbing

Sources of Receiving Prophetic Revelation

and terrifying dreams and visions. Often, we ignore them without taking the appropriate action in the Spirit realm. This type of dream is God exposing the attacks, plots and schemes by the devil that can be eradicated and thwarted by the prayer of faith. You may ask, "Why do I really need the dream? Why do I need to know what the devil is doing?" You see, knowing this is very helpful, because it will help to ignite your heart to wage war in the Spirit against the plans of the enemy. Instead of being afraid, depressed or discouraged in the attack, you can instead stand boldly and condemn the strategy and plot of the enemy.

God promises that in the last days He will pour out His Spirit upon all flesh; that our sons and daughters will prophesy and the young men will see visions and the old men will dream dreams. This is our confidence that we are in the last hour and that God is actually pouring out His Spirit. It is very important that you learn how to make the distinction between the dreams that are from God and those that are not, so that you may be able to interpret your dreams.

KEYS TO INTERPRETING DREAMS

Let's look at some keys that will help open the door to the interpretation of the dreams that God may give to you. Mind you, these are just "some" keys.

The first key is that you must have a one-to-one relationship with your Father. You must be in relationship with God and walking in His commandments to be able to understand what He is saying through dreams. The more depth you have with God, the more you'll become sharp and sensitive in understanding His Voice. If you don't have an ongoing relationship with God, you cannot have depth in the things of God. And if you don't have depth in the things of God, it becomes impossible to properly discern the Voice of God in dreams.

> **Yea, if thou criest after knowledge, and liftest up thy voice for understanding;**
>
> **If thou seekest her as silver, and searchest for her as for hid treasures;**
>
> **Then shalt thou understand the fear of the LORD, and find the knowledge of God.**
>
> **Proverbs 2:3-5**

The second key is that you must be ready and willing to research and investigate the symbols and sayings of the dream

Sources of Receiving Prophetic Revelation

or revelation you receive. Many times, when we have a dream, it comes predominantly in symbols. Sometimes it does not come very clearly. This can be frustrating. If you really want to understand the meaning of the dream you receive and thereby know what God is saying to you, you must be ready to study and research the symbols of the dream. This is not for lazy people. Lazy Christians always want someone else to interpret their dreams for them. They are too lazy to take the time to research for themselves the meaning of the symbols in their dreams. The Bible says "If you call out for insight and cry aloud for understanding, and if you look for it as for silver and search for it as for hidden treasure, then you will understand the fear of the Lord and find the knowledge of God." This is the promise of God for us. Let's take advantage of it.

The third key is that whenever you receive a dream, the first thing you must do is to ask God if the dream is for you or for someone else. Many times, when you receive a dream, it can be for someone else in your family, among your friends, co-workers and church family or even someone with whom you're not familiar. It is important that you find who the dream is for, before you start panicking unnecessarily. People panic and become depressed and discouraged over dreams that are meant for others. The reason they feel this way is because they think it was for them. Be very careful and sensible in interpreting what you have seen. Don't even force an interpretation or try to make it fit a predetermined opinion or desire.

Finally, learn to honor others as you share what you have seen in your dream. Be ready and prepared to submit what you have seen and what you think it means to others who can help you arrive at a truthful and objective interpretation and thereby bring clarity to you.

HOW TO BE PREPARED TO RECEIVE A DREAM OR A VISION FROM GOD

I sleep, but my heart waketh: it is the voice of my beloved that knocketh, saying, Open to me, my sister, my love, my dove, my undefiled: for my head is filled with dew, and my locks with the drops of the night.

Song of Solomon 5:2

Often, you hear Christians say that they desire for God to speak to them in dreams and visions. Yet, they are not ready and prepared to receive when the dream or vision comes. It is important that we are in a ready posture or in a readiness of mind when we receive a dream or a vision. But how do we do

Sources of Receiving Prophetic Revelation

that?

> **And I say unto you, Ask, and it shall be given you; seek, and ye shall find; knock, and it shall be opened unto you.**
>
> **For every one that asketh receiveth; and he that seeketh findeth; and to him that knocketh it shall be opened.**
>
> **If a son shall ask bread of any of you that is a father, will he give him a stone? or if he ask a fish, will he for a fish give him a serpent?**
>
> **Or if he shall ask an egg, will he offer him a scorpion?**
>
> **If ye then, being evil, know how to give good gifts unto your children: how much more shall your heavenly Father give the Holy Spirit to them that ask him?**
>
> **Luke 11:9-13**

First, ask the Lord to speak to you while you sleep and EXPECT Him to do it. Jesus said, "Ask and it shall be given to you." All you need to do is just ask with a sincere heart that God will speak to you while you sleep and He will.

Second, be willing, prepared and ready to wake up no matter how late in the night or in the morning to write down the things God reveals to you. Often, when God speaks to us in a dream or in a vision while we are sleeping, we get too lazy to wake up to write down what He reveals to us. Some of us just wake up and fall back to sleep. Yet you say that you want God to speak to you while you are asleep. There is a responsibility we must undertake when God speaks to us while we are asleep. We must train ourselves to be disciplined so as to be able to wake up and write down whatever God is revealing to us. Never be so lazy that you cannot treasure the Word of the Lord. One very important way to avoid laziness is not to eat too much before you go to bed. When you are filled up with food before going to bed, it makes it difficult for you to remember and receive what God is revealing to you.

Many of us have often awakened from a vivid dream in the middle of the night, thinking that we will remember it when the morning comes. When you do that, you will find yourself with a vague recollection of what the Lord had shown to you. This is why you must seize the moment.

Third, make a habit of keeping a pen and note pad at your bedside to inscribe those things you may receive, see and hear in your dreams and visions.

Finally, learn to make a note of your thoughts about the

dream at the time. Then, when you awaken in the morning, you are then able to read it clearly and study it through to its interpretation. The very act of doing this will cause you to become more sensitive to hearing and receiving from the Lord while you sleep, which in turn will enable Him to speak more frequently to you this way.

VISIONS

Visions are another channel or source through which God can speak to His people today. Sometimes God can speak and lead a believer through a vision. There are three kinds of visions. The first kind is called the spiritual vision. The second kind is the vision which is received through a trance and the third kind is the open vision.

The spiritual vision is the vision that involves the ability to see into the Spirit realm. You are able to see with the eyes of your spirit. This has nothing to do with the physical eyes.

The second vision occurs when a believer falls into a trance. When a believer falls into a trance, his physical senses are suspended. In other words, they are not in charge of their physical senses. The spiritual senses take over. He or she is not unconscious; he or she is just unaware of his vicinity. He or she is more spiritually conscious than physically conscious.

The open vision is different. This is when all of your senses are intact. You can see the vision with your physical eyes. Your senses are not suspended. But the great difference is that only the individual sees what is going on. Nobody else within their surroundings sees what is going on except with the permission of the Spirit of God.

> **After these things the word of the LORD came unto Abram in a vision, saying, Fear not, Abram: I am thy shield, and thy exceeding great reward.**
>
> **And Abram said, Lord GOD, what wilt thou give me, seeing I go childless, and the steward of my house is this Eliezer of Damascus?**
>
> **And Abram said, Behold, to me thou hast given no seed: and, lo, one born in my house is mine heir.**
>
> **And, behold, the word of the LORD came unto him, saying, This shall not be thine heir; but he that shall come forth out of thine own bowels shall be thine heir.**

Sources of Receiving Prophetic Revelation

And he brought him forth abroad, and said, Look now toward heaven, and tell the stars, if thou be able to number them: and he said unto him, So shall thy seed be.

Genesis 15:1-5

Abram had a vision and received the Word of the Lord. Obviously, this was not a spiritual vision or a trance. Abram had an open vision. His senses were intact. They were not suspended. He knew in the vision that he was childless. If his senses were suspended, then he would not have known. But he knew what was going on around him. He knew that he had a steward named Eleazar. Abram was able to respond back to God in the vision and hold a conversation. This experience is not just for Abraham. God is doing the same thing today for all who will not limit Him. God wants also to speak and lead His people through visions. He desires to send His Word through any avenue He wills. We must not limit God. We will have visions like never before in these last days. But visions will come to those who believe that God still speaks through visions. They will not come to "doubting Thomases" or to the rigid, starchy and religious believers. They will only come to the sons of God that have been truly manifested in this hour. There are sons of God that have not yet been manifested and there are others who have. God is still waiting and yearning for His manifested sons.

> **And God spake unto Israel in the visions of the night, and said, Jacob, Jacob. And he said, Here am I.**
>
> **And he said, I am God, the God of thy father: fear not to go down into Egypt; for I will there make of thee a great nation:**
>
> **I will go down with thee into Egypt; and I will also surely bring thee up again: and Joseph shall put his hand upon thine eyes.**
>
> **Genesis 46:2-4**

Jacob, called Israel, had a vision in Beersheba when he came to offer sacrifices to God. He had an open vision in which God communicated with him. It is a beautiful thing for God to communicate to His people. God is still communicating with His people. Words of direction and prosperity were given to Jacob through visions. God, through a vision, will give new direction and leading to His people. There are many believers whose call was confirmed through a vision or a dream. I am not talking about man-made dreams and visions. I am referring to the God-inspired, God-given and God-directed vision and dream.

Sources of Receiving Prophetic Revelation

And it came to pass that night, that the word of the LORD came unto Nathan, saying,

Go and tell my servant David, Thus saith the LORD, Shalt thou build me an house for me to dwell in?

Now therefore so shalt thou say unto my servant David, Thus saith the LORD of hosts, I took thee from the sheepcote, from following the sheep, to be ruler over my people, over Israel:

I will be his father, and he shall be my son. If he commit iniquity, I will chasten him with the rod of men, and with the stripes of the children of men:

But my mercy shall not depart away from him, as I took it from Saul, whom I put away before thee.

And thine house and thy kingdom shall be established for ever before thee: thy throne shall be established for ever.

II Samuel 7:4,5,8,14,15,16

The prophet Nathan had a similar experience. He had a vision from God, not for himself, but for King David. The Lord can give us a vision for someone other than ourselves. God spoke to the prophet Nathan in a vision confirming David's kingdom through his sons, promising eternal mercy and kingdom to the house of David. This is what God can do through a vision. We can receive accurate Words of the Lord from a vision for our brothers and sisters. Visions are not meant to heap glory and praise upon ourselves. We must never become conceited or develop a "big head," for the dreams and visions are an act of God.

God knows us better than we know ourselves. He will not give a vision to someone just so he can go and proclaim "I just heard from God!" Instead, God will give a vision or speak to those He knows will follow Him out of obedience. It is only as we develop a faithful and obedient heart, that God can trust us to hear Him when He speaks.

God is looking for those to whom He can speak in the midnight hour and say, "Go and lay your hands on that sister," and they will obediently get out of bed and go straight to that sister's house. God does not give an individual a vision or a dream or even speak to an individual so they can go around rejoicing how wonderful it is that God spoke to them. God will only give visions, dreams and instructions to an individual that will be obedient to His Voice once he or she hears it.

Sources of Receiving Prophetic Revelation

Again, let's look at visions in the New Testament.

And he became very hungry, and would have eaten: but while they made ready, he fell into a trance,

And saw heaven opened, and a certain vessel descending unto him, as it had been a great sheet knit at the four corners, and let down to the earth:

Wherein were all manner of fourfooted beasts of the earth, and wild beasts, and creeping things, and fowls of the air.

And there came a voice to him, Rise, Peter; kill, and eat.

Now while Peter doubted in himself what this vision which he had seen should mean, behold, the men which were sent from

Cornelius had made inquiry for Simon's house, and stood before the gate,

Acts 10:10-13,17

Peter fell into a trance, which is another form of vision. As we said earlier, what at times is seen and heard in a vision is symbolic. It takes the Spirit of God to properly interpret a symbol. That is why it is important not to share your vision with just anybody. It should only be shared with people whom the Spirit of the Lord specifies. They should be men and women that are gifted in properly interpreting your vision.

Peter saw heaven open and he saw a certain vessel descending to him. In other words, Peter saw things that he could not understand. Many of us have visions and dreams like that. We see things that we cannot understand. We cannot tell what it means. We cannot even relate to it. So what we do is, we just abandon the vision or dream in our minds. It is important that we learn to write our visions and dreams in a diary, whether we understand them or not. This is necessary because sometime in the future, you will be surprised how that vision or dream will unfold before your eyes.

Peter could not understand his trance. The Bible says that Peter was perplexed concerning the meaning of the trance. He literally was unable to interpret his vision. While he was still pondering about it, the interpretation was made clear when Peter arrived at the house of Cornelius, who was a Gentile. Peter said in verse 28, "You know that it is an unlawful thing for a man that is a Jew to keep company, or come unto one of another nation; but God has shewed me that I should not call any man common or unclean."

Sources of Receiving Prophetic Revelation

ANOTHER DIMENSION

Where there is no vision, the people perish: but he that keepeth the law, happy is he.

Proverbs 29:18

Without a prophetic vision the people perish. Another translation says, "Without a prophetic vision, the people cast off restraint, without a prophetic vision, the people cast off discipline, and without a prophetic vision, the people wander in darkness." Where there is a prophetic vision, there is a harness directive. I believe that in the last days, God will raise up young men that have visions for the Body of Christ to bring restraint upon the Body of Christ and to mobilize us to the will of God.

I believe old men will rise up with dreams. We often talk about how Martin Luther King, Jr. stood up and said, "I have a dream." What was it? Do you believe it was something that came to him in the night? Do you believe it was something that came before him in a trance? No. I believe it was the quickening power of God that wanted to use a man to reveal the destiny of a nation, to break down strife, to break sectarianism, to break down racism and bring a nation into the

Prophetic Development

position of divine unity.

So there is another whole aspect where God can release a purpose in a man and the man can rise up and say, " I have a dream and the dream will come upon the people for restraint and for discipline to bring the people together." The fulfillment of Acts 2:14 rests upon us. It does not rest upon some mystical time clock out in the heavens somewhere. It rests upon a generation that will arise and take upon themselves the restraint and the discipline of the Holy Spirit to prepare for the last day visitation of God's Spirit and glory.

GUIDELINES FOR INTERPRETING DREAMS, VISIONS AND TRANCES

Dreams, visions and trances come to us in symbolic forms. Seldom do they come to us plain and clear without any symbolic meaning. The majority of dreams, visions and trances come in symbols, and because of this it is very important to understand the guidelines for interpreting them.

The first step is to rightly determine which elements or parts of the dream, vision or trance are meant to be interpreted as symbolic. If the picture or language of the dream, vision or trance makes no literal or actual sense, then it must be

Sources of Receiving Prophetic Revelation

interpreted as having symbolic sense. If it does make literal or actual sense or meaning, then it can only be interpreted as having symbolic sense or meaning when the dream, vision or trance implies or relates to other dreams, visions or trances that you have had.

Second, the interpreter of the dream, vision and trance must be able to recognize the three fundamental elements of symbolic interpretation. That is, the significance of a symbol is based upon the literal or actual nature and characteristic of that which is being used as a symbol. A symbol is meant to represent something different than itself. The interpreter must understand that the link between that which is used as a symbol and that which is symbolized is the characteristic common to both.

Third, the interpreter must keep in mind that something may be used to symbolize more than one thing in a dream, vision or a trance. The same symbol may represent different aspects of a characteristic. For example, the picture of gold is used to represent divine nature, wisdom or faith. Also some symbols may have good and evil aspects to them. For example, the lion is used as a symbol of Jesus, His saints and also the devil in Revelation 5:5 and I Peter 5:8. Symbols often have negative and positive or good and bad applications. For

Prophetic Development

example, birds, such as the dove or raven, symbolize spirits. The dove is symbolic of the Holy Spirit and the raven is symbolic of the evil spirit, yet both are birds. Remember, there is one interpretation but many applications of symbols. It is worth remembering that satan is the great counterfeiter of all that God does. He is not an originator, but a counterfeiter. God is the originator of all things, while satan counterfeits all that God does. The true believer is not to let the error of cultic symbolism rob him of the truth of divine symbolism. The Bible provides safe guidelines for principles of interpretation of those symbols which the believer should follow. This will prevent you from falling into any counterfeit symbolism or false allegories in your dream, vision or trance.

CHAPTER 2

PROPHETIC INTERPRETATION AND UNDERSTANDING

No man, when he hath lighted a candle, covereth it with a vessel, or putteth it under a bed; but setteth it on a candlestick, that they which enter in may see the light.

For nothing is secret, that shall not be made manifest; neither any thing hid, that shall not be known and come abroad.

Take heed therefore how ye hear: for whosoever hath, to him shall be given; and whosoever hath not, from him shall be taken even that which he seemeth to have.

Luke 8:16-18

When we give forth prophetic revelation knowledge, we are giving forth light and dispelling darkness. When prophetic knowledge comes, light also comes with it and darkness concerning that thing is immediately dispelled. A man with no revelation knowledge is an enemy of Israel– the Church.

God has two ways of speaking. He gives you prophetic revelation knowledge, which must be immediately released. Then He gives you secrets, which must be kept and later released in due time. A secret given, when released at the wrong time, can cause destruction, division, confusion and persecution.

The secret of the LORD is with them that fear him; and he will shew them his covenant.

Psalm 25:14

It is clear that God has some secrets and mysteries. It is not for everyone. It is only for those who fear Him. In fact, the Scripture says that "it is with them that fear Him." In other words, if you are looking for the secrets and mysteries of God, you can only find them in and from men and women who fear God and not from individuals who are walking in their own ways. Be careful who you go to for counseling and advice. Men and women with the fear of God always have God's secrets and mysteries to unlock the solution to your problem.

TAKING HEED TO WHAT YOU HEAR

If any man have ears to hear, let him hear.

And he said unto them, Take heed what ye hear: with what measure ye mete, it shall be measured to you: and unto you that hear shall more be given.

For he that hath, to him shall be given: and he that hath not, from him shall be taken even that which he hath.

Mark 4:23-25

We must take heed how we hear and how we prophetically interpret and understand the word of the Lord given to us. This has been a great problem to many individuals in the Body of Christ. Many believers have prophetically misinterpreted and misunderstood prophetic words that were spoken over them. Because of this, many believers at times blame the prophets for giving them a wrong word. They wonder why the words spoken by the prophet did not come to pass. One of the great causes of this is that we have men and women who prophetically misinterpret and misunderstand the word of the Lord that is given to them. We must learn to hear and comprehend prophetically when God speaks. Many times we hear incorrectly and think what we

Prophetic Development

hear is right.

We must discern by the Spirit of God concerning what God is saying when we receive a promise or a word of the Lord. We must not assume. We must learn to find out the underlying point.

Let's go back again to Mark 4:23-25.

If any man have ears to hear, let him hear.

And he said unto them, Take heed what ye hear: with what measure ye mete, it shall be measured to you: and unto you that hear shall more be given.

For he that hath, to him shall be given: and he that hath not, from him shall be taken even that which he hath.

Mark 4:23-25

This Scripture will give you a proper understanding of what is being said here and will also increase your ability to receive from God.

The word "hear" in verse 23 as we understand it does not convey the full meaning of the word our Lord originally spoke. The word He used is the Greek word AKOUO. The primary meaning of this word is *to hear with understanding*.

And he called the multitude, and said unto them, Hear, and understand:

Matthew 15:10

This Scripture properly brings clarity to the original meaning of the word "hear" as it was used by Jesus. The words from Mark's gospel should have been translated in the same way– to hear and understand. It is important for us not only to hear the word of the Lord given to us, but our hearing must be accompanied by proper understanding and interpretation. So verse 23 of Mark 4 can then be read like this: "If any man has ears to hear and understand, let him understand." God does not just want us to hear, but He wants us to understand what we are hearing.

Jesus warned us to be careful of what we hear and understand. It is a solemn warning that we must take very seriously. We must hear prophetically so that we can understand and interpret prophetically.

Prophetic Development

And He said to them, Be careful what you are hearing. The measure [of thought and study] you give [to the truth you hear] will be the measure [of virtue and knowledge] that comes back to you, and more [besides] will be given to you *who hear.*

Mark 4:24 (AMP)

And He was saying to them, "Take care what you listen to. By your standard of measure it shall be measured to you; and more shall be given to you besides.

Mark 4:24 (NAS)

Jesus said that with whatever measure of understanding you have, your ability to receive will be either expanded or limited. If you understand little, you will receive little. If you understand much, you will receive much. The more you understand, the more you can receive.

With him will I speak mouth to mouth, even apparently, and not in dark speeches; and the similitude of the LORD shall he behold: wherefore then were ye not afraid to speak against my servant Moses?

Numbers 12:8

Prophetic Interpretation and Understanding

God at times speaks to us in dark sayings. This is when you don't understand what God is saying to you or when you cannot figure out immediately what God is trying to say. When a dark saying or speech is received or given, the individual is supposed to meditate and pray about it for a clear understanding of what God is saying. Many of us make great mistakes in this area. We prefer to ask people about the meaning of what has been spoken to us. Nobody can better understand the promise of God for your life than you. Many of those we go to for interpretation of the promises given to us may not even know their left from their right. They may interpret it without fully understanding the promise. Why? Because it does not belong to them.

Dark speeches and sayings come in two forms. The first form is when a word is given to you and only you know what it means. Nobody else in your household, among your friends, church or clique knows it. Just you and God. The second form is when God speaks to you and you don't understand it at all. This is when you cannot figure out what the word is about. When this happens, the first thing to do is not to neglect or disregard the word of the Lord given to you simply because you cannot understand it. Instead, you need to meditate on it and pray for the proper interpretation.

Then Martha, as soon as she heard that Jesus was coming, went and met him: but Mary sat still in the house.

Then said Martha unto Jesus, Lord, if thou hadst been here, my brother had not died.
But I know, that even now, whatsoever thou wilt ask of God, God will give it thee.

Jesus saith unto her, Thy brother shall rise again.
Martha saith unto him, I know that he shall rise again in the resurrection at the last day.

Jesus said unto her, I am the resurrection, and the life: he that believeth in me, though he were dead, yet shall he live:

And whosoever liveth and believeth in me shall never die. Believest thou this?

John 11:20-26

This is a good example of how a person can receive a word from the Lord and misunderstand its meaning. Sometimes, some things in our lives need to die so that God can speak prophetically into our beings to produce a resurrection. Jesus wanted Lazarus to die because the glory of his resurrection would be greater than the glory of his healing.

Prophetic Interpretation and Understanding

What I want you to note very carefully is how Martha heard the words from Jesus and misinterpreted them. This is exactly what we do. Jesus told Martha that her brother Lazarus "shall rise again," yet Martha did not understand the meaning of the prophetic word that was given to her. Martha, like many Christians today, misunderstood the season that the promise was made for. She thought that Jesus was talking about the final resurrection at the last day. Because Martha did not understand the prophetic promise spoken by Jesus, she was unable to take heed to what was spoken.

Martha misinterpreted the prophecy given to her. She said "I know that he shall rise again in the resurrection at the last day." When we receive a word of prophecy or when a word is spoken over us, we must not be quick to interpret it. Allow the Spirit of God to open your understanding and make the interpretation clear. Many Christians have run out of meetings, conferences and churches with misinterpreted words of prophecy. A misinterpreted word will not produce any fruit or result. It is not surprising that many individuals complain of promises not coming to pass in their lives.

Jesus said, Take ye away the stone. Martha, the sister of him that was dead, saith unto him, Lord, by this time he stinketh: for he hath been dead four days.

Jesus saith unto her, Said I not unto thee, that, if thou wouldest believe, thou shouldest see the glory of God?

John 11:39-40

When Jesus told Martha to move the stone, Martha's reply again showed that she did not understand the word of the Lord given to her by Jesus that her brother will rise again. Martha's reply was "Lord, by this time he stinketh." Jesus had to remind her of the prophetic promise which was given to her.

HOW TO DEVELOP PROPHETIC INTERPRETATION AND UNDERSTANDING

The first important principle in developing prophetic understanding is that we must **learn to seek the Lord**.

Evil men understand not judgment: but they that seek the LORD understand all things.

Proverb 28:5

Seeking the Lord brings understanding and clarity concerning His ways.

Prophetic Interpretation and Understanding

The second principle is that we must **shun evil**.

> **Many shall be purified, and made white, and tried; but the wicked shall do wickedly: and none of the wicked shall understand; but the wise shall understand.**
>
> **Daniel 12:10**

The Bible makes it clear that none of the wicked shall understand. That is to say, when we begin to walk in disobedience and out of the will of God, understanding and proper interpretation of the things of God become rare and scarce. Only the wise shall "understand." Wisdom comes to people that fear God. The word "fear" here is not the fear that brings torment, but reverential fear.

The third principle is that we must **learn to walk in the rhythm of faith**.

> **Now faith is the substance of things hoped for, the evidence of things not seen.**
>
> **For by it the elders obtained a good report.**
>
> **Through faith we understand that the worlds were framed by the word of God,**

Prophetic Development

so that things which are seen were not made of things which do appear.

Hebrews 11:1-3

So then faith cometh by hearing, and hearing by the word of God.

Romans 10:17

Walking by faith produces understanding of the things of God.

The fourth principle is **study the Word of God**.

Study to shew thyself approved unto God, a workman that needeth not to be ashamed, rightly dividing the word of truth.

II Timothy 2:15

The final principle is **pray the prayer of the Apostle Paul**.

Wherefore I also, after I heard of your faith in the Lord Jesus, and love unto all the saints,

Prophetic Interpretation and Understanding

Cease not to give thanks for you, making mention of you in my prayers;

That the God of our Lord Jesus Christ, the Father of glory, may give unto you the spirit of wisdom and revelation in the knowledge of him:

Ephesians 1:15-17

We must realize that understanding and interpretation are within our grasp.

CHAPTER 3

GROWING IN THE PROPHETIC ANOINTING

But covet earnestly the best gifts: and yet shew I unto you a more excellent way.

I Corinthians 12:31

For we know in part, and we prophesy in part.

I Corinthians 13:9

But he that prophesieth speaketh unto men to edification, and exhortation, and comfort.

He that speaketh in an unknown tongue edifieth himself; but he that prophesieth edifieth the church.

I Corinthians 14:3-4

This is the desire of most Christians. There is the hunger to develop and increase their level of the prophetic flow. It is the Lord Who must sovereignly anoint, equip, and use a person in any realm of prophecy. But there are some very important principles which can be followed to prepare ourselves and to develop the prophetic anointing upon our lives.

> **And when Paul had laid his hands upon them, the Holy Ghost came on them; and they spake with tongues, and prophesied.**
>
> **Acts 19:6**

> **And the same man had four daughters, virgins, which did prophesy.**
>
> **Acts 21:9**

> **And it shall come to pass afterward, that I will pour out my spirit upon all flesh; and your sons and your daughters shall prophesy, your old men shall dream dreams, your young men shall see visions:**
>
> **And also upon the servants and upon the handmaids in those days will I pour out my spirit.**
>
> **Joel 2:28-29**

> **And there was one Anna, a prophetess, the daughter of Phanuel, of the tribe of Aser: she was of a great age, and had**

lived with an husband seven years from her virginity;

Luke 2:36

But this is that which was spoken by the prophet Joel;

And it shall come to pass in the last days, saith God, I will pour out of my Spirit upon all flesh: and your sons and your daughters shall prophesy, and your young men shall see visions, and your old men shall dream dreams:

And on my servants and on my handmaidens I will pour out in those days of my Spirit; and they shall prophesy:
And I will shew wonders in heaven above, and signs in the earth beneath; blood, and fire, and vapour of smoke:

Acts 2:16-19

But every woman that prayeth or prophesieth with her head uncovered dishonoureth her head: for that is even all one as if she were shaven.

I Corinthians 11:5

The first principle is to believe that prophecy was a vital part of the early church ministry. And if it is true, prophecy is supposed to be a vital part of the present day New Testament church. Prophecy brings the fire of Pentecost to the church meetings. Prophecy flows from the spirit.

The second principle is learning to release the faith to prophesy. Faith is very important for prophecy because one can only speak forth in this way based on his proportion of faith. Faith is a gift from God, but it is like a mustard seed planted in each person's life that needs to grow every day. To increase your faith for this realm, you must constantly hear and study the Word of God, because only through the Word does faith arise. With a dynamic prayer and Word life depositing the seed of the Word within your heart, you are in a good position to have God quicken that Word and to cause faith to arise to prophesy what the Lord has given.

He taught me also, and said unto me, Let thine heart retain my words: keep my commandments, and live.

Proverb 4:4

Third, learn how to receive a Word from the Lord. The Spirit will give a word to a person by means of a single word, a sentence, a spiritual burden, a vision or a spiritual thought that gives a quickening of joy to the person at the time. A word of prophecy is not just a passing good thought or idea. It is a quickened Spirit-anointed burden and Word from the

Lord that gives its recipient a definite feeling of the need for its expression. The Word that the Lord gives should always edify, exhort or comfort the people of God.

The fourth principle is learning to move out at the right time in a meeting. The Holy Spirit expresses different moods in different meetings. The Christian who believes that he has a prophetic word for the church must ask himself about the mood of the Spirit in the meeting, before moving out in prophetic utterance. It is possible that the word the person has received from the Lord is only for himself or for a later time. These things must be properly discerned in every meeting by the person who believes that he has a prophetic word. A good way to learn how to move out at the right time is to observe when the more mature and seasoned prophetic ministries operate. To start prophesying during the opening announcements or when someone is speaking would be unedifying and out of order.

Another principle is to develop the ability to discern your own thoughts and feelings from those of the Holy Spirit. It is very important that we don't project our preconceived thoughts and ideas into the prophetic stream. This caution is not to put us into the bondage of fear whereby we refuse to function in the liberty of the Spirit. We learn to prophesy just

Prophetic Development

as a child learns to walk. It takes a number of falls before we can walk steadily by ourselves. If a person is going through some specific problem or emotional anxiety, you may have the tendency to prophesy these things. For example, if you are moved upon by the Holy Spirit to give someone a gift and you have not yet done this, you might project what the Spirit was saying to you upon the congregation by saying words like, "For surely the Lord is calling you or us to a greater level of giving." In doing this, you are putting your own thoughts, dealings, needs, problems, and questions on someone or on the congregation.

This is unanointed, unedifying and unfortunate for the people. The Old Testament refers to men that do this as false prophets who "prophesy out of their own heart and visions." You must remember that our thoughts can sometimes come from God, ourselves and the devil. It is not beyond a Spirit-filled Christian to speak the wrong words. We are human and liable to error.

For us to make our hearts and minds more accessible to the Spirit, we must (a) cleanse and transform our minds daily through the Word of God (Romans 12:1-3); and (b) we must learn to bring every thought into obedience to Jesus Christ (II Corinthians 10:1-6). Having a clean heart and a transformed mind will allow the Holy Spirit to easily bring forth a clear, spiritual word of prophecy.

> **But covet earnestly the best gifts: and yet shew I unto you a more excellent way.**
>
> **II Corinthians 12:31**

The next principle is cultivating a hunger for spiritual gifts. Many Christians and local churches do not function freely in spiritual gifts because they do not have a Godly desire to see them operate. Without an earnest thirst for the Spirit to operate the gifts in the church, the church will not see the manifestation of the power of God. The word "covet" means "to have a strong desire toward." God wants us to have a healthy hunger after spiritual gifts.

> **My soul cleaveth unto the dust: quicken thou me according to thy word.**
>
> **Plead my cause, and deliver me: quicken me according to thy word.**
>
> **Psalm 119:25, 154**

And you hath he quickened, who were dead in trespasses and sins;

Even when we were dead in sins, hath quickened us together with Christ, (by grace ye are saved;)

Ephesians 2:1, 5

For Christ also hath once suffered for sins, the just for the unjust, that he might bring us to God, being put to death in the flesh, but quickened by the Spirit:

I Peter 3:18

It is the spirit that quickeneth; the flesh profiteth nothing: the words that I speak unto you, they are spirit, and they are life.

John 6:63

Another principle to growing in the prophetic flow is receiving the quickening of the Holy Spirit. The word "quickening" means "to make alive" and "to give life." A person who prophesies or flows in the prophetic anointing must learn how to be quickened in his own spirit by the Holy Spirit. The quickening of the Spirit is the very breath of this ministry. The Spirit will give the thoughts of the Lord to the congregation.

SENSITIVITY TO THE PROPHETIC SPIRIT

Before you begin to prophesy, you will usually sense to some degree the anointing of God upon your life. As you respond to this anointing and step out by faith with a prophetic utterance, the Holy Spirit will increase your prophetic anointing. However, as soon as the Holy Spirit's message has been adequately communicated, the person prophesying will sense a lifting or a lessening of the prophetic unction. It is important at this time for the person to be sensitive to the leading of the Spirit and prepare to stop when the Spirit ceases to enable him to flow forth.

> **And for me, that utterance may be given unto me, that I may open my mouth boldly, to make known the mystery of the gospel,**
>
> **For which I am an ambassador in bonds: that therein I may speak boldly, as I ought to speak.**
>
> **Ephesians 6:19-20**

Another important principle is the knowledge of how to begin speaking in the prophetic spirit. Getting started in a prophetic flow is probably the most difficult part of moving in prophecy. Yet, the more you do it, the easier it becomes. Your first step must be taken in boldness and faith. The word "bold" is used in the New Testament approximately sixteen times and it means to act with unexpected or seemingly extreme conduct, to set out with a definite goal, to dare to do something and to lose all fear of something. When you prophesy, you must lose all fear of yourself, of others present, of the possibility of mispronouncing words, missing the correct prophetic flow, prophesying uninspired words from the devil and operating in a strange unknown realm. Be sensitive to the presence of God upon you. This sensitivity to God's presence upon you will enable you to be bold in a gentle and humble way.

Finally, determine to cultivate self-control and temperance in the operation of the prophetic gift. Many times people who are operating in the prophetic for the first time, or who are young in the things of the Spirit, become so excited at sensing the anointing of God's Spirit upon their lives that they tend to lose self-control and may even become fanatical in their expression of the prophetic flow. When you prophesy, you must realize that you are in control of your expressions and emotions. God anoints, but He does not overpower. God moves, but He moves in a wise way. Everyone that operates in the prophetic realm should learn to control his gift along with its expression. He should also learn to give place to the next person and prefer him in honor. When there is self-control and temperance in the ministry of the prophetic gift, each local church can be greatly edified.

CHAPTER 4

THE WAYS OF DELIVERING PROPHETIC WORDS

God, who at sundry times and in divers manners spake in time past unto the fathers by the prophets,

Hebrews 1:1

The phrase "at sundry times and in divers manners" was written in the Greek *polumeros kai polutropos*, a familiar literary form of Greek alliteration. It literally means "in many pasts and in many ways." Each prophet contributed various parts of prophetic revelation and this was done in many varied ways. The prophets received revelation from God in order that they would deliver their messages to the people as they had received them. These many ways can be placed under three categories in which the prophets conveyed their messages.

Prophetic Development

REVELATION THROUGH
THE RELEASE OF WORDS

Most prophetic revelation was often delivered through the verbal mode of delivery.

And Elijah the Tishbite, who was of the inhabitants of Gilead, said unto Ahab, As the LORD God of Israel liveth, before whom I stand, there shall not be dew nor rain these years, but according to my word.

I Kings 17:1

And the LORD sent Nathan unto David. And he came unto him, and said unto him, There were two men in one city; the one rich, and the other poor.

The rich man had exceeding many flocks and herds:

But the poor man had nothing, save one little ewe lamb, which he had bought and nourished up: and it grew up together with him, and with his children; it did eat of his own meat, and drank of his own cup, and lay in his bosom, and was unto him as a daughter.

And there came a traveller unto the rich man, and he spared to take of his own flock and of his own herd, to dress for the wayfaring man that was come unto him; but took the poor

man's lamb, and dressed it for the man that was come to him.

And David's anger was greatly kindled against the man; and he said to Nathan, As the LORD liveth, the man that hath done this thing shall surely die:

And he shall restore the lamb fourfold, because he did this thing, and because he had no pity.

And Nathan said to David, Thou art the man. Thus saith the LORD God of Israel, I anointed thee king over Israel, and I delivered thee out of the hand of Saul;

And I gave thee thy master's house, and thy master's wives into thy bosom, and gave thee the house of Israel and of Judah; and if that had been too little, I would moreover have given unto thee such and such things.

Wherefore hast thou despised the commandment of the LORD, to do evil in his sight? thou hast killed Uriah the Hittite with the sword, and hast taken his wife to be thy wife, and hast slain him with the sword of the children of Ammon.

Now therefore the sword shall never depart from thine house; because thou hast despised me, and hast taken the wife of Uriah the Hittite to be thy wife.

Prophetic Development

Thus saith the LORD, Behold, I will raise up evil against thee out of thine own house, and I will take thy wives before thine eyes, and give them unto thy neighbour, and he shall lie with thy wives in the sight of this sun.

For thou didst it secretly: but I will do this thing before all Israel, and before the sun.

And David said unto Nathan, I have sinned against the LORD. And Nathan said unto David, The LORD also hath put away thy sin; thou shalt not die.

Howbeit, because by this deed thou hast given great occasion to the enemies of the LORD to blaspheme, the child also that is born unto thee shall surely die.

And Nathan departed unto his house. And the LORD struck the child that Uriah's wife bare unto David, and it was very sick.

David therefore besought God for the child; and David fasted, and went in, and lay all night upon the earth.

And the elders of his house arose, and went to him, to raise him up from the earth: but he would not, neither did he eat bread with them.

And it came to pass on the seventh day, that the child died.

The Ways of Delivering Prophetic Words

And the servants of David feared to tell him that the child was dead: for they said, Behold, while the child was yet alive, we spake unto him, and he would not hearken unto our voice: how will he then vex himself, if we tell him that the child is dead?

But when David saw that his servants whispered, David perceived that the child was dead: therefore David said unto his servants, Is the child dead? And they said, He is dead.

Then David arose from the earth, and washed, and anointed himself, and changed his apparel, and came into the house of the LORD, and worshipped: then he came to his own house; and when he required, they set bread before him, and he did eat.

Then said his servants unto him, What thing is this that thou hast done? thou didst fast and weep for the child, while it was alive; but when the child was dead, thou didst rise and eat bread.

And he said, While the child was yet alive, I fasted and wept: for I said, Who can tell whether GOD will be gracious to me, that the child may live?

But now he is dead, wherefore should I fast? can I bring him back again? I shall go to him, but he shall not return to me.

Prophetic Development

And David comforted Bathsheba his wife, and went in unto her, and lay with her: and she bare a son, and he called his name Solomon: and the LORD loved him.

And he sent by the hand of Nathan the prophet; and he called his name Jedidiah, because of the LORD.

And Joab fought against Rabbah of the children of Ammon, and took the royal city.

And Joab sent messengers to David, and said, I have fought against Rabbah, and have taken the city of waters.

Now therefore gather the rest of the people together, and encamp against the city, and take it: lest I take the city, and it be called after my name.

And David gathered all the people together, and went to Rabbah, and fought against it, and took it.

And he took their king's crown from off his head, the weight whereof was a talent of gold with the precious stones: and it was set on David's head. And he brought forth the spoil of the city in great abundance.

And he brought forth the people that were therein, and put them under saws, and under harrows of iron, and under axes

of iron, and made them pass through the brickkiln: and thus did he unto all the cities of the children of Ammon. So David and all the people returned unto Jerusalem.

II Samuel 12:1-31

SPOKEN WORD. Prophetic revelation might be delivered in a spoken word, as seen in Elijah's prophecy to Ahab, or in Nathan's prophecy to David.

WRITTEN WORD. The prophetic message might also be delivered through the written word, as seen in the books of Isaiah, Jeremiah and Daniel. The majority of the prophets' revelation differed in style of expression, emphasis and intensity. Their words were often highly figurative and poetic.

THE LANGUAGE OF THE PROPHETS. The prophets' language included the following kinds of speech: riddles, parables, allegory, metaphors and similes. One of the most outstanding characteristics of prophetic delivery is symbolism. Daniel is probably the most graphic Old Testament example. In a presbytery, the prophetic word may at times came forth from the prophets in similar language of parables, metaphors, similes or the like. This kind of prophetic language serves to convey more clearly in pictorial imagery what God is saying to the candidates. Other times, the prophetic word can be plain and direct.

For unto us a child is born, unto us a son is given: and the government shall be upon his shoulder: and his name shall be called Wonderful, Counsellor, The mighty God, The everlasting Father, The Prince of Peace.

Isaiah 9:6

THE PROPHETIC PERFECT. The Hebrew language of the Old Testament has only two tenses, the perfect and the imperfect. These two tenses do not entirely parallel our English tenses, which regard tense in the sense of time. Rather, the Hebrew people considered the completion or incompletion of the action as important. The perfect tense indicated that the action was completed, while the imperfect indicated that the action was still to be completed. When the prophets prophesied about some future event, they would often use the tense of completed action, the perfect tense. The prophet was stating a predictive word as an already accomplished event. This procedure was the result of the spirit of faith of the prophet, who was so certain of the fulfillment of his word that he stated it as an already accomplished event.

One of the best known examples is the example of the

Scripture, when he predicted the future birth of Christ, "for unto us a child is born... ." In the Hebrew, the prophetic perfect literally reads, "a child has been born." Yet, this event would not be fulfilled for over seven centuries.

REVELATION THROUGH THE PROPHET'S LIFE

Then said the LORD unto me, Go yet, love a woman beloved of her friend, yet an adulteress, according to the love of the LORD toward the children of Israel, who look to other gods, and love flagons of wine.

So I bought her to me for fifteen pieces of silver, and for an homer of barley, and an half homer of barley:

Hosea 3:1-2

Revelation was also conveyed not only by words but also by the life of the prophet. The Prophet Hosea was married to a harlot to symbolize the spiritual adultery of unfaithful Israel. The life experience of Hosea symbolizes Israel's apostasy. The Prophet Hosea lived out the prophetic message of the tender love and forgiving compassion of Jehovah toward Israel. Hosea's life with Gomer was a prophetic parable in history of the Lord Who would one day save His unfaithful wife by purchasing her from slavery, shame and sin.

REVELATION THROUGH
THE PROPHETIC ACTIONS

The symbolic acts of the prophets were also vehicles for delivering divine revelation. The prophetic act was itself as much a mode of divine revelation as was the prophet's words. The symbolic act was a graphic means of gaining the attention of the people, and dramatizing God's message to them.

> **In the year that Tartan came unto Ashdod, (when Sargon the king of Assyria sent him,) and fought against Ashdod, and took it;**
>
> **At the same time spake the LORD by Isaiah the son of Amoz, saying, Go and loose the sackcloth from off thy loins, and put off thy shoe from thy foot. And he did so, walking naked and barefoot.**
>
> **And the LORD said, Like as my servant Isaiah hath walked naked and barefoot three years for a sign and wonder upon Egypt and upon Ethiopia;**
>
> **So shall the king of Assyria lead away the Egyptians prisoners, and the Ethiopians captives, young and old, naked**

and barefoot, even with their buttocks uncovered, to the shame of Egypt.

And they shall be afraid and ashamed of Ethiopia their expectation, and of Egypt their glory.

And the inhabitant of this isle shall say in that day, Behold, such is our expectation, whither we flee for help to be delivered from the king of Assyria: and how shall we escape?

Isaiah 20:1-6

The Prophet Isaiah walked naked and barefoot to symbolize the similar fate awaiting Egypt and Ethiopia from Assyria in Jeremiah chapters 27 and 28. The Prophet Jeremiah walked through the streets wearing a yoke around his neck to signify future Babylonian bondage.

And Ahijah caught the new garment that was on him, and rent it in twelve pieces:

I Kings 11:30

The Prophet Ahijah tore Jeroboam's garment into twelve pieces, thus symbolizing the dividing of the kingdom. And in the New Testament, in Acts 21:11, the Prophet Agabus bound his own hands and feet with Paul's girdle, thus depicting the future binding of Paul at Jerusalem. Symbolic acts of prophets can happen today. However, such acts would be more the exception and not the norm. In a presbytery, prophetic revelation will mostly come through the mode of prophetic words, not acts.

CHAPTER 5

GUIDELINES FOR PROPHETIC MINISTRATIONS

We not only need to stir and release the prophetic ministry, we also need to understand the guidelines for channeling this flow properly. There are always those who will misuse and abuse the freedom of the Spirit. In the Old Testament, Samuel established a school of prophets. The school of the prophets made teaching available to the younger prophets in training. This teaching was a combination of the Law of Moses, the history of Israel, the covenants given to the people of the Lord, and the practical principles of living as a prophet. Most of the younger prophets would be discipled by a veteran prophet for the impartation of truth through God by example.

The prophetic ministry is not such that a person can receive the anointing to prophesy through teaching, but he can receive teachings on how to properly channel and operate the prophetic gift he possesses. Anyone that is functioning or that desires to function in the prophetic ministry, congregational prophecy, prophetic "song of the Lord" needs to have these guidelines by which to carefully examine himself. The flow of God's Spirit must remain pure and unpolluted by human pride, egotism or other works of the flesh. It is possible to have the right attitudes and desires in our hearts, but wrong practices when moving in the prophetic. And so we really need to understand some safety tips that will enable us to flow properly in the prophetic anointing.

> **Examine yourselves, whether ye be in the faith; prove your own selves. Know ye not your own selves, how that Jesus Christ is in you, except ye be reprobates?**
>
> **II Corinthians 13:5**

The first safety tip is, always be sure that you are ministering from the right motivation. The word "motivation" means an inner drive that causes one to act in a certain way. It is an inner impulse. Everyone has motivations. Some of the motivations are good and some are bad. Because of our Adamic nature with its desires, its carnal habits, and its selfish motivations, we must examine ourselves and be honest before the Lord and with ourselves, in order to discern our true motivations. Always ask yourself, "Why do you do the things you do? Or, "What force is driving you to do the things that you do? Do you move in the prophetic to prove your spirituality? Do you move in the prophetic to be seen by others and receive recognition and praise? Do you move in the prophetic to be like some man of God we admire and want to be identified with? Do you move in the prophetic to establish your ministry as a prophet and thus receive more authority and recognition?"

Put not forth thyself in the presence of the king, and stand not in the place of great men:

Proverb 25:6

A man's gift maketh room for him, and bringeth him before great men.

Proverb 18:16

He loveth transgression that loveth strife: and he that exalteth his gate seeketh destruction.

Proverb 17:19

The Book of Proverbs is known as the Book of Wisdom or the Book for Right Living. There is wisdom in the above Scriptures that, when we adhere to it, will protect us from undue harm. The Scripture in Proverb 25:6 says that we must not put forth ourselves in the presence of the king. This speaks of pushing ourselves forward to be seen or honored. The thought here is to avoid carnal ambition. Also, in Proverb 18:16, God promises that your gift will make room for you. If a person possesses a gift of God, he need not be concerned about acceptance or recognition. The gift will cause people to open themselves to the ministry of the prophet. The motivation in us that we must always examine is self-ambition. Am I bringing attention to myself and my gift? Or do I rest in the principles of God?

In Proverb 17:19, the Bible admonishes us that he that exalteth his gate seeketh destruction. In Scripture, the gate was symbolic of a man's position in the city as one of the decision makers, leaders or elders. The Bible instructs us not to exalt our own leadership or ministry because destruction of both gift and person will result. The prophetic gift is not to be used by self-ambitious people to establish their own reputations. We must not be driven by our reputation, nor by the dictates of our Adamic nature. Instead, we should gently yield to the Holy Spirit.

The second safety tip is to be mindful not to monopolize the prophetic ministry in the corporate gatherings. To monopolize simply means "to secure and retain exclusive possession or control of something, to take advantage of a privilege so as to have control." The prophetic ministry is for the Body of Christ to be edified and encouraged. Most churches which have a strong prophetic flow also have a free-flowing style of worship and response to the Lord. Within this kind of atmosphere where ministry to the Lord and to one another is encouraged, there is the possibility of people misusing or taking advantage of the openness of the meetings. The leadership of the church is responsible for setting guidelines that will protect the flow of the Spirit of God in the worship service.

In every congregation there always seem to be people who feel they are the mouthpiece of the Lord for every meeting. Taking advantage of the corporate gathering of God's people should be corrected by the local leadership. There must be a clear discernment between being moved by individual personalities or by the anointing of God. Some people have an outgoing personality and have no fear of speaking in a public meeting, while others with a more self-conscious personality have great difficulty in speaking out. If the local leadership does not correct those who are monopolizing, the shy ones with a true word from God may never speak unto the Body of Christ.

And he shewed me a pure river of water of life, clear as crystal, proceeding out of the throne of God and of the Lamb.

Revelation 22:1

Finally, don't allow mixture in the prophetic ministry. The word "mixture" means that which consists of different ingredients blended without order, that which contains two or more elements, that which is confused or muddled." Whenever we are moving in the gifts of the Holy Spirit, there is the possibility of mixture. Mixture in the prophetic ministry means whatever would pollute the pure flow of the Holy Spirit in the prophetic word. This could be created from carnality, sensuality, hidden habits, personality weaknesses, wrong motivations and emotional stress.

Mixture comes when we blend together the feelings and words of our soul with the words and anointing of the Holy Spirit. Mixture is something we must all deal with. The vessel who is to be used by the Lord must maintain his purity. It is our responsibility to keep our hearts, minds and spirit clean and ready to respond to the Word.

Guidelines for Prophetic Ministrations

PROPHETIC ETIQUETTE

As we move in the spiritual gifts, there are always areas in which we should be careful. The following are just some things that we need to be careful of and try to avoid when operating in the prophetic ministry.

(a) Don't speak so softly that no one can hear the words that you are saying.

(b) Don't speak so swiftly that no one can understand the word.

(c) Don't speak so long that no one can remember the first part of the word.

(d) Don't speak the same word as the previous speaker. There is a difference in speaking confirmation and being redundant.

(e) Don't speak harsh condemnation and judgment against the local church.

(f) Don't speak with distracting mannerisms that draw attention to yourself rather than the word.

Prophetic Development

(g)   Don't speak so many times that you monopolize the church meeting.

CHAPTER 6

POSITIONING FOR THE PROPHETIC WORD

And he spake many things unto them in parables, saying, Behold, a sower went forth to sow;

And when he sowed, some seeds fell by the way side, and the fowls came and devoured them up:

Some fell upon stony places, where they had not much earth: and forthwith they sprung up, because they had no deepness of earth:

And when the sun was up, they were scorched; and because they had no root, they withered away.

And some fell among thorns; and the thorns sprung up, and choked them:

But other fell into good ground, and brought forth fruit, some an hundredfold, some sixtyfold, some thirtyfold.

Who hath ears to hear, let him hear.

And the disciples came, and said unto him, Why speakest

thou unto them in parables?

He answered and said unto them, Because it is given unto you to know the mysteries of the kingdom of heaven, but to them it is not given.

For whosoever hath, to him shall be given, and he shall have more abundance: but whosoever hath not, from him shall be taken away even that he hath.

Therefore speak I to them in parables: because they seeing see not; and hearing they hear not, neither do they understand.

And in them is fulfilled the prophecy of Esaias, which saith, By hearing ye shall hear, and shall not understand; and seeing ye shall see, and shall not perceive:

For this people's heart is waxed gross, and their ears are dull of hearing, and their eyes they have closed; lest at any time they should see with their eyes, and hear with their ears, and should understand with their heart, and should be converted, and I should heal them.

But blessed are your eyes, for they see: and your ears, for they hear.

For verily I say unto you, That many prophets and righteous men have desired to see those things which ye see, and have

Positioning for the Prophetic Word

not seen them; and to hear those things which ye hear, and have not heard them.

Hear ye therefore the parable of the sower.

When any one heareth the word of the kingdom, and understandeth it not, then cometh the wicked one, and catcheth away that which was sown in his heart. This is he which received seed by the way side.

But he that received the seed into stony places, the same is he that heareth the word, and anon with joy receiveth it;

Yet hath he not root in himself, but dureth for a while: for when tribulation or persecution ariseth because of the word, by and by he is offended.
He also that received seed among the thorns is he that heareth the word; and the care of this world, and the deceitfulness of riches, choke the word, and he becometh unfruitful.

But he that received seed into the good ground is he that heareth the word, and understandeth it; which also beareth fruit, and bringeth forth, some an hundredfold, some sixty, some thirty.

Matthew 13:3-23

Prophetic Development

The prophetic word could be likened to a seed that must fall on the ground and then bring forth fruit. The analogy of the Word of God being likened to the seed is taught throughout the Scriptures. In Matthew 13:3-23, Jesus speaks of the four attitudes of the heart which are represented by the four kinds of soil the seed could fall upon. Believers will respond to a prophetic word with the same four heart attitudes.

The first kind of soil speaks of the heart which is not given to cultivate the Word of God in the midst of the busy routines of life. The wayside was the path alongside the roads and highways between cities, the roads used in everyday life. A seed falling on this ground would be on top of the earth, not being able to sprout as a seed that has fallen on farming ground. The seed does not penetrate the person's understanding because he is given to the natural mind, to the ways of the world. He is not seeking after God's Word or bringing God into the routine of his daily life. It is not that he has a major deterrent in his life to the ways of God, he simply has no desire or time to follow the Lord.

The second kind of soil speaks of the hard heart which has no roots of Christ-like character. In this type of soil, the Word takes root, but because the ground is stony– loose and gravelly– the roots cannot take hold and form a strong root structure. The believer receives the Word with initial enthusiasm and joy, and it begins to grow within him. But when trials come, he is easily swayed and the Word is uprooted. These two ses contain two very important principles in receiving a word from the Lord. First of all, people receiving prophetic words must understand that its fulfillment depends as much on the power of the prophetic word received as it does on the heart condition of the receiver. If you have no character roots and no depth of integrity, if your heart is hard and shallow, then the word sowed into your life will dwell within us only temporarily.

A hard heart will not allow a person to become rooted in the word. He will only allow the word to touch the areas of his personality which he permits. The word is obstructed by not giving the Lord free course through his being.

The second important principle in verse 21 is that when affliction and persecution arise because of the Word, immediately the Word can fall away. Whenever we receive a word from the Lord, we receive the potential for that word to be tested and tried, and therefore affliction and persecution will arise in your life. If we have no roots in ourselves or strength to wage a good warfare with the word received, in times of affliction and persecution, the word will immediately fall away from us. We must cultivate a heart that has character and strength that can retain the good words the Lord would sow among us.

The third soil is the heart attitude of incomplete surrender to the Lordship of Jesus Christ. There is nothing wrong with the seed, but if the soil is not cultivated it cannot bring forth the seed. Hearts must be prepared and cultivated so that the word received from God will not be choked out or stunted in its growth. When the spirit of this world has not been weeded out of our heart ground, the thorns of deceitfulness and materialism, the thorns of anxiety and worry will choke out the prophetic word and it cannot produce fruit.

There is nothing wrong with the prophetic word that has been sown into his life. The problem is that he did not tear down and destroy the thorns and the thistles that were dwelling within his heart to make room for the good Word of God to bring forth fruit. He has not taken consideration to remove from his life those things which compete against the Word of God.

The fourth kind of soil is the good heart that understands the Word. This is the soil of a good and honest heart. The word "honest" in Greek means "sound or healthy, praiseworthy, pure, without hypocrisy or pretension." The good soil is the honest heart of a man who can hear the Word of God and understand it. When we cultivate such a heart attitude of honesty and integrity, we will receive the seed of the Word of God and it will bring forth fruit every time without error.

> **Every good gift and every perfect gift is from above, and cometh down from the Father of lights, with whom is no variableness, neither shadow of turning.**
>
> **Of his own will begat he us with the word of truth, that we should be a kind of firstfruits of his creatures.**
>
> **Wherefore, my beloved brethren, let every man be swift to hear, slow to speak, slow to wrath:**
>
> **For the wrath of man worketh not the righteousness of God.**
>
> **Wherefore lay apart all filthiness and superfluity of naughtiness, and receive with meekness the engrafted word, which is able to save your souls.**
>
> **But be ye doers of the word, and not hearers only, deceiving your own selves.**
>
> **For if any be a hearer of the word, and not a doer, he is like unto a man beholding his natural face in a glass:**

Prophetic Development

For he beholdeth himself, and goeth his way, and straightway forgetteth what manner of man he was.

But whoso looketh into the perfect law of liberty, and continueth therein, he being not a forgetful hearer, but a doer of the work, this man shall be blessed in his deed.

James 1:17-25

For this cause also thank we God without ceasing, because, when ye received the word of God which ye heard of us, ye received it not as the word of men, but as it is in truth, the word of God, which effectually worketh also in you that believe.

I Thessalonians 2:13

In the above verses, the Apostle James gives us the account of a man receiving a good word from the Lord. When we receive a prophetic word from the Lord, it is a God gift coming forth from the Father, Who can only give what is good. In verse 21, James says that by receiving the word with meekness and humility, it will be able to change you and even to save you from great destruction and disaster. In I Thessalonians 2:13, Paul gives us a very important principle. We are to accept the prophetic word, not as the word of men, but as the Word of God which is able to work in us and perform in you the good will of the Father.

CHAPTER 7

UNDERSTANDING THE TRANSFERENCE OF PROPHETIC WORDS OF PROMISE TO A GENERATION

Wherefore (as the Holy Ghost saith, To day if ye will hear his voice,

Harden not your hearts, as in the provocation, in the day of temptation in the wilderness:

When your fathers tempted me, proved me, and saw my works forty years.

Wherefore I was grieved with that generation, and said, They do alway err in their heart; and they have not known my ways.

So I sware in my wrath, They shall not enter into my rest.)

Prophetic Development

Take heed, brethren, lest there be in any of you an evil heart of unbelief, in departing from the living God.

But exhort one another daily, while it is called To day; lest any of you be hardened through the deceitfulness of sin.

For we are made partakers of Christ, if we hold the beginning of our confidence stedfast unto the end;

While it is said, To day if ye will hear his voice, harden not your hearts, as in the provocation.

For some, when they had heard, did provoke: howbeit not all that came out of Egypt by Moses.

But with whom was he grieved forty years? was it not with them that had sinned, whose carcases fell in the wilderness?

And to whom sware he that they should not enter into his rest, but to them that believed not?

So we see that they could not enter in because of unbelief.

Hebrews 3:7-19

It is so important that we understand the generational transference of God's promise. An important principle to note in understanding this is that a "promise given not received still remains." That is to say, when God gives us a promise and the promise is not embraced or received, such promise still remains. The promise is transferred to another generation of the individual. And if by chance the second generation refuses to receive the promise, it is again transferred to the third generation. This continues until a member of the generation receives and embraces the promise. The word of the Lord does not return to God void until His assignments and functions are completed.

> **How long shall I bear with this evil congregation, which murmur against me? I have heard the murmurings of the children of Israel, which they murmur against me.**
>
> **Say unto them, As truly as I live, saith the LORD, as ye have spoken in mine ears, so will I do to you:**
> **Your carcases shall fall in this wilderness; and all that were numbered of you, according to your whole number, from twenty years old and upward, which have murmured against me,**
>
> **Doubtless ye shall not come into the land, concerning which I sware to make you dwell therein, save Caleb the son of Jephunneh, and Joshua the son of Nun.**
>
> **But your little ones, which ye said should be a prey, them will I bring in, and they shall know the land which ye have despised.**

Prophetic Development

But as for you, your carcases, they shall fall in this wilderness.

And your children shall wander in the wilderness forty years, and bear your whoredoms, until your carcases be wasted in the wilderness.

After the number of the days in which ye searched the land, even forty days, each day for a year, shall ye bear your iniquities, even forty years, and ye shall know my breach of promise.

Numbers 14:27-34

God gave the children of Israel a promise. The promise was that He was going to take them to a land that flows with milk and honey. It was a word from the Lord to the Israelites. But because of their laziness, their murmuring, their complaining and their lack of commitment, the promise of God was transferred to another generation. It is important that we understand that when God gives us a promise– a word– He expects us to participate in bringing it to pass.

In the above scripture, the Lord called the Israelites an evil congregation. Why? Because of their murmuring, laziness and lack of commitment in "entering in." Then the Lord said "Ye shall not come into the land concerning which I sware to make you dwell therein." You might wonder, why is God changing His mind when He promised that He was going to take them to the Promised Land? That is why we need to understand the generational transference of God's promise. God is not withdrawing His promise. His word is still Yea and Amen. His word or promise will not return to Him void without fulfilling what it is sent to accomplish.

What is happening here is a key principle which we have neglected for a long time. We think once a word of the Lord is given to us, we can just act any way we want to and expect it to come to pass. Many Christians think God is magical. God is not and will never be magical. He is a procedural God. In other words, He allows man to participate in His operation.

God did not withdraw the promise from the children of Israel. He just transferred the promise from one generation to the other. Verse 31 says "But your little ones, which ye said should be a prey, them will I bring in, and they shall know the Lord which ye despised." God was transferring the promise of one generation to the other. When God gives you a "promise" or a "word," you must "enter in." The promise is from God, but the "entering in" is your responsibility. When God promises you that you are going to become a great musician, that does not mean that it must come to pass. It is optional.

Prophetic Development

You have to learn to "enter in" to the promise for it to be manifested. Many Christians are never ready to "enter in" to their promise and possess what God has said. They always want someone else to "enter in" for them.

> **And see the land, what it is; and the people that dwelleth therein, whether they be strong or weak, few or many;**
>
> **And what the land is that they dwell in, whether it be good or bad; and what cities they be that they dwell in, whether in tents, or in strong holds;**
>
> **And what the land is, whether it be fat or lean, whether there be wood therein, or not. And be ye of good courage, and bring of the fruit of the land. Now the time was the time of the firstripe grapes.**
>
> **And they went and came to Moses, and to Aaron, and to all the congregation of the children of Israel, unto the wilderness of Paran, to Kadesh; and brought back word unto them, and unto all the congregation, and shewed them the fruit of the land.**
>
> **And they told him, and said, We came unto the land whither thou sentest us, and surely it floweth with milk and honey; and this is the fruit of it.**

> **Nevertheless the people be strong that dwell in the land, and the cities are walled, and very great: and moreover we saw the children of Anak there.**
>
> **The Amalekites dwell in the land of the south: and the Hittites, and the Jebusites, and the Amorites, dwell in the mountains: and the Canaanites dwell by the sea, and by the coast of Jordan.**
>
> **Numbers 13:18-20, 26-29**

Now let us look at these Scriptures carefully. I believe that it will shed some light on what I am talking about. As I said earlier, God promised Moses and the Israelites that He was going to give them a land. Not just an ordinary land; it was a land that was to flow with milk and honey. This means that God was promising them that He was going to lead them to a place where all of their needs would be met. There is no better "promise" or "word" than that. God promised that they would become the new landlord of Canaan. It was a promise which God was ready to back. But a promise is not meaningful until it is received. Moses and the children of Israel had to "enter in" to the promise.

Often, when you are "entering in" to God's promise for your life, you will have to encounter the existing giants of the land. Most Christians are too timid to fight. They don't want to confront the enemies of their promise and of their soul. We must learn and be ready to dispossess in order to possess what God has for us. We must be ready to drive out all of the squatters from the land of our promise and be prepared to take it by force.

Moses sent out folks among his congregation to spy out the land. He wanted to have a glimpse of God's promise. He wanted to know the content of the land. He wanted to know the kind of people inhabiting the land. He wanted to know the kinds of fruit and vegetables in the land, and he wanted to find out how much honey was in the land. Spying out the land of our promise should always increase our craving to possess it and our readiness to pay the necessary price. It should not be an avenue to quit and fail. The report produced after the spying or after having a glimpse of the land confirms God's promise of the land being full of milk and honey. They loved what they saw. They loved the land.

THE GIANTS IN YOUR PROMISE

Nevertheless the people be strong that dwell in the land, and the cities are walled, and very great: and moreover we saw the children of Anak there.

> **The Amalekites dwell in the land of the south: and the Hittites, and the Jebusites, and the Amorites, dwell in the mountains: and the Canaanites dwell by the sea, and by the coast of Jordan.**
>
> **But the men that went up with him said, We be not able to go up against the people; for they are stronger than we.**
>
> **Numbers 13:28-29, 31**

The children of Israel would love to be the new landlord of the land– the promise of God. But there was only one problem: They did not know how to "enter in" to the promise. They were afraid to possess God's promise for their lives and generation because of the giants in the land. Many of us sometimes want the easy way out. We always want a promise or a land that is inhabited or guarded by grasshoppers. We want to wake up and find that all of a sudden the promise of God for our lives has come to pass. God prefers to give us promises that are inhabited and guarded by giants. Our God is a Giant Killer, if we believe it. God's word or promises are precious. When a word is spoken over us, we must be ready to "enter in" to the promise and possess it. Let's not wait for it to come to us. We must go to the promise.

Prophetic Development

And Caleb stilled the people before Moses, and said, Let us go up at once, and possess it; for we are well able to overcome it.

Numbers 13:30

And Joshua the son of Nun, and Caleb the son of Jephunneh, which were of them that searched the land, rent their clothes:

And they spake unto all the company of the children of Israel, saying, The land, which we passed through to search it, is an exceeding good land.

If the LORD delight in us, then he will bring us into this land, and give it us; a land which floweth with milk and honey.

Only rebel not ye against the LORD, neither fear ye the people of the land; for they are bread for us: their defence is departed from them, and the LORD is with us: fear them not.

Numbers 14:6-9

Only two of the men that went to spy the land were prepared to "enter in" to God's promise for their lives. Despite the giants in the promise of their land, Caleb and Joshua were still confident that they were able to possess the promise of

God for their lives. They were what I call "water walking Christians." They were ready to take God at His word. They were confident of the Greater One in them than the giants in the land. They had a different attitude, and for this they were able to possess the promise of God. As long as you are scared of giants possessing your promise, you will never receive a manifestation of it. God is not going to drive out the giants for you. All He does is give you the promise. It is our responsibility to dispossess the giants in our promise so that we can possess it. We have many Christians who have received

the "word of the Lord"— the promise of God— but none of these promises seemed to be coming to pass because they were not ready to drive out the giants from their land.

THREE KINDS OF CHRISTIANS

There are three kinds of Christians in the Body of Christ today:

(1) the Risk Taker
(2) the Caretaker
(3) the Undertaker

The Risk Takers are the group of Christians that are prepared to take risks at the word of the Lord— the promise of God. They are not afraid to fail and make mistakes.

The Caretakers are the kind of Christians who like to take care of other people's problems and never take care of their own. The Caretaker will always want to sort out your life for you and never likes to sort out his own life.

Last, the Undertakers are the kind of Christians who love to destroy your ministry, your call and your vision. They are always available to dry up your zeal for the Lord and His work. The strategy of the Undertakers is they use other Christians, preferably other disobedient Christians, to get the job done. The Undertakers never have confidence in what you are doing. They are always wishing doom, not openly but in the secret of their hearts, for almost every project or thing you do.

TWO FORMS OF GENERATIONAL TRANSFERENCE OF GOD'S PROMISE

Therefore, while the promise of entering His rest still holds and is offered [today], let us be afraid [to distrust it], lest any of you should think he has come too late *and* has come short

of [reaching] it.

For indeed we have had the glad tidings [of God] proclaimed to us just as truly as they [the Israelites of old did when the good news of deliverance from bondage came to them]; but the message they heard did not benefit them, because it was not mixed with faith [that is, with the leaning of the entire personality on God in absolute trust and confidence in His power, wisdom and goodness] by those who heard it; *neither were they united in faith with* [Joshua and Caleb] the ones who heard [did believe].

Hebrews 4:1-2 (AMP)

Therefore, since the promise of entering his rest still stands, let us be careful that none of you be found to have fallen short of it. 2 For we also have had the gospel preached to us, just as they did; but the message they heard was of no value to them, because those who heard did not combine it with faith.

Hebrews 4:1-2 (NIV)

The first form is when a "promise" or a "word of the Lord" is given to a generation for *another* generation. This happens when God gives a "word of promise" to one generation, but it is being fulfilled in the other generation. An example is when

Prophetic Development

God gives a word of promise to a father concerning his unborn grandchild, that the child will be a great vessel for His kingdom. In this case, the word of promise is given to the father of what will take place with his unborn grandchild. The fulfillment of the word is for another generation. When the child is born, the child unknowingly begins to find himself fulfilling the word of promise that was spoken over his grandfather for his life. I strongly believe that many of us in the Body of Christ today are living out some of the words of promise given to our previous generations for us without our knowing.

> **And as since the time that I commanded judges to be over my people Israel, and have caused thee to rest from all thine enemies. Also the LORD telleth thee that he will make thee an house.**
>
> **And when thy days be fulfilled, and thou shalt sleep with thy fathers, I will set up thy seed after thee, which shall proceed out of thy bowels, and I will establish his kingdom.**
>
> **He shall build an house for my name, and I will stablish the throne of his kingdom for ever.**
>
> **I will be his father, and he shall be my son. If he commit iniquity, I will chasten him with the rod of men, and with the stripes of the children of men:**

> **But my mercy shall not depart away from him, as I took it from Saul, whom I put away before thee.**
>
> **And thine house and thy kingdom shall be established for ever before thee: thy throne shall be established for ever.**
>
> **II Samuel 7:11-16**

This is a good example of the first form of generational transference of God's promise. God spoke to the prophet Nathan, after David had shown a desire to build God a house, and God then gave Nathan "words of promise" for David. Even though the words were given to David, it was actually for his seed. It was for a different generation and not for his generation. Now watch this. God gave a word of promise to David saying "I will set up thy seed after thee, which shall proceed out of thy bowels, and I will establish his kingdom and he shall build me an house for my name ... ." God was giving David a word which would be transferred to his generation— which is seed. Even though the word was given to him, it was for his generation.

> **And Hiram king of Tyre sent his servants unto Solomon; for he had heard that they had anointed him king in the room of his father: for Hiram was ever a lover of David.**

And Solomon sent to Hiram, saying,

Thou knowest how that David my father could not build an house unto the name of the LORD his God for the wars which were about him on every side, until the LORD put them under the soles of his feet.

But now the LORD my God hath given me rest on every side, so that there is neither adversary nor evil occurrent.

And, behold, I purpose to build an house unto the name of the LORD my God, as the LORD spake unto David my father, saying, Thy son, whom I will set upon thy throne in thy room, he shall build an house unto my name.

I Kings 5:1-5

This Scripture shows us God's words of promise being fulfilled. The word given to David which were transferred to his generation is seen here fulfilled in the life of his son Solomon. King Solomon in his message to Hiram king of Tyre repeated and demonstrated the fulfillment of the word of the Lord spoken over his father David. He said "And, behold, I purpose to build an house unto the name of the Lord my God, as the Lord spake unto David my father, saying thy son shall build an house ... ." This is a generational transference of God's promise.

The second form of transference is when a "word of promise" is given to a specific generation. In a first generation— because of laziness, lack of discipline, commitment and a refusal to "enter in" to the promise— the promise did not come to pass. The word of promise is then transferred to another generation, say a second generation belonging to the same lineage of the first generation. The word of promise remains in the generation until someone receives it. If no one receives it, the word of promise will continually be transferred from one generation to the other, until someone in that generation has the guts to receive it. As long as it is not received, it will remain in that generation. It will not return to God void. It must return with the assignment completed. When God gives a word, He does not take it back. Once God speaks a word, the word is <u>not allowed</u> to return without fulfilling what it was sent to do.

HOW TO "ENTER IN" TO GOD'S PROMISE

For as the rain cometh down, and the snow from heaven, and returneth not thither, but watereth the earth, and maketh it bring forth and bud, that it may give seed to the sower, and bread to the eater:

So shall my word be that goeth forth out of my mouth: it shall not return unto me void, but it shall accomplish that which I please, and it shall prosper in the thing whereto I sent it.

Isaiah 55:10-11

There are some important keys that must be considered in order to properly understand how to "enter in" to God's promise for your life.

First, you must be willing to dispossess the images that are of no value in your mind and install images of value in the throne of your mind.

Casting down imaginations, and every high thing that exalteth itself against the knowledge of God, and bringing into captivity every thought to the obedience of Christ;

II Corinthians 10:5

There are things that have been set in our minds—mindsets. If you are ever going to enter into your promise, you must be willing to destroy the mindsets. The word "imaginations" here in the original means "images of no value." When God gives us a word of His promise concerning any area of our lives, the first thing to do is to dispossess the original images that are of no value, that are already in us and that may counter the promise given to us. For example, if a word of promise is given to you saying that God will give you a child or will heal you of cancer, in order to be able to receive that promise you must first dispossess the existing images of defeat, fear, death, doubt, impossibility and failure. These images are of no value. You have to first of all cast them down, and maintain them cast down, and then be willing to install in the throne of your mind new images that are of value— images that match the promise of God for your life.

If you do not dispossess the old images which are of no value, they will constantly choke and resist the word of promise. They will cause you to doubt and operate in unbelief. Unbelief simply means "not fully convinced." Images that are of no value will cause an individual not to be fully convinced concerning God's promise. And if you stay not convinced of God's promises, you will never see the manifestation of the promise of God.

Second, God's promise for our lives must be mixed with faith and with hope.

For unto us was the gospel preached, as well as unto them: but the word preached did not profit them, not being mixed with faith in them that heard it.

Hebrews 4:2

The gospel of God is the promise of God. When a word of the Lord is given to us, it is God's promise that is given to us. God's promise for our lives can only come to pass when the promise is mixed with faith. The apostle Paul let us know that the promise made to the Israelites did not come to pass because the promise given when received was not mixed with faith. If it was not mixed with faith, it must then be mixed with unbelief, which means that they were not fully convinced or persuaded of God's promise.

What is desire? It is a longing and craving for the choice of God for your life. *The third important key is that you must learn to fall in love with God's desire. This is very crucial to entering into God's promise. Your promise from God will always be barren until you learn to fall in love with God's desire. When God's desire becomes your desire, the promise of God for your life will then be fruitful.* Your promise will not produce any spiritual fruit until you fall in love with God's desire for your life. Then you can begin to

Understanding the Transference of Prophetic Words of Promise to a Generation

experience fruitfulness.

> **And Jacob went out from Beersheba, and went toward Haran.**
>
> **And he lighted upon a certain place, and tarried there all night, because the sun was set; and he took of the stones of that place, and put them for his pillows, and lay down in that place to sleep.**
>
> **And he dreamed, and behold a ladder set up on the earth, and the top of it reached to heaven: and behold the angels of God ascending and descending on it.**
>
> **And, behold, the LORD stood above it, and said, I am the LORD God of Abraham thy father, and the God of Isaac: the land whereon thou liest, to thee will I give it, and to thy seed;**
>
> **And thy seed shall be as the dust of the earth, and thou shalt spread abroad to the west, and to the east, and to the north, and to the south: and in thee and in thy seed shall all the families of the earth be blessed.**
>
> **And, behold, I am with thee, and will keep thee in all places whither thou goest, and will bring thee again into this land; for I will not leave thee, until I have done that which I have spoken to thee of.**

And Jacob awaked out of his sleep, and he said, Surely the LORD is in this place; and I knew it not.

Genesis 28:10-16

Jacob, while on his way to Padanaram, stopped at a "certain place" and decided to take a short nap. While he was sleeping, the Lord gave him a word of promise in a dream. Jacob actually received the word of the Lord. ***The Lord gave him a promise that he was going to become a great nation.*** Now watch this. Even though Jacob's nature had not yet been changed, God still gave him an awesome word of promise.

Jacob wakes up from his sleep excited and saying that God is going to make him a great nation. He was so thrilled and excited over the word of the Lord— the word of promise. This is exactly our reaction when a word of promise is given to us. We get thrilled over the word of promise, hoping it comes to pass. Jacob after his excitement said let me go and find a woman so that I can become a great nation.

RACHEL— MY DESIRE

Rachel was Jacob's desire. Rachel was not God's desire. God's desire for Jacob was Leah. Many times we fall into this same predicament. We see a great ministry or a great work and because it is all together and attractive, we immediately say to ourselves, "Well, this is where God will launch me." We always try to force our desire on God. We need to continually check our desire to make sure that it is not our "Rachel." Rachel is symbolic of our desire. Leah is symbolic of God's desire for our lives. It was not through Rachel that he was going to become father of many nations. It was through Leah.

Even though Leah was present in the same house with Rachel, Jacob could not even look at her because he was consumed with his desire— Rachel. Until our desire dies, God's desire for our lives will never manifest. We must always see our Leahs before our Rachels. Jacob was more in love with HIS desire than with God's desire. He was more concerned about the day he was going to marry Rachel, how Rachel was going to give him children, how he was going to have a great ministry, and how he was going to be known and popular.

LEAH— GOD'S DESIRE FOR YOUR LIFE

The seven years he spent working to receive Rachel passed like days because he was madly in love. Many times we don't mind spending time with our desire because we are in love with it. But God has a way of giving us His desire anyway. After serving for seven years, Jacob was deceived. Instead of Rachel, Leah was given to him. He was made to serve another seven years for Rachel. What Jacob did not realize was that Laban was giving him God's desire. The very one who would actually help him to build and fulfill the ministry God had promised him— the father of many nations.

Your desire will always be barren until you fall in love with God's desire. When God's desire becomes your desire, your desire will be fruitful. Rachel, Jacob's desire, was barren and could not have a child. Rachel was not the source to fulfill God's call and purpose on Jacob's life. Leah was to be the source where His ministry and calling would be birthed. Again, it is important to remember that when God promises to make you into anything, the first thing to do is to fall in love with His desire and not your desire.

The fourth key to understand in "entering in" to God's promise is that we must be able to "see the promise."

And when the LORD saw that Leah was hated, he opened her womb: but Rachel was barren.

And Leah conceived, and bare a son, and she called his name Reuben: for she said, Surely the LORD hath looked upon my affliction; now therefore my husband will love me.

Genesis 29:31-32

Once you fall in love with God's desire, God gives you spiritual insight to see the direction He is leading you into. He begins to open up the vision to your understanding.

SIMEON - TO HEAR

The next key to entering in to God's promise is to hear.

And she conceived again, and bare a son; and said, Because the LORD hath heard that I was hated, he hath therefore given me this son also: and she called his name Simeon.

Genesis 29:33

Hearing produces faith to make one able to fulfill God's desire. After receiving spiritual insight into the word "received," we need to also continuously operate or stay in faith concerning the word. The spirit of unbelief must die. You keep on reminding yourself of the "word" received and the faithfulness of God toward the promise. Your faith will then always be at a higher level.

Prophetic Development

LEVI - TO JOIN AND ATTACH

Another key is that we must be willing to "attach" and be "joined" to God's desire.

And she conceived again, and bare a son; and said, Now this time will my husband be joined unto me, because I have born him three sons: therefore was his name called Levi.

Genesis 29:34

Jacob was now attached and joined to God's desire. This is exactly what happens when a word is received. After the stage of having spiritual insight into the word and then continuously hearing God's word to build our level of confidence, we must then be connected, joined and attached to the word which was given to us and which is God's desire for our lives.

Finally, we must be willing to praise God for the promise.

JUDAH - PRAISE

And she conceived again, and bare a son: and she said, Now will I praise the LORD: therefore she called his name

Judah; and left bearing.

Genesis 29:35

You will not be able to show God's praise until you have a spiritual insight of the word of promise, until your confidence level of the promise is high, and until you are joined and attached to God's desire.

THE FULFILLMENT OF OUR DESIRE

And afterwards she bare a daughter, and called her name Dinah.

And God remembered Rachel, and God hearkened to her, and opened her womb.

And she conceived, and bare a son; and said, God hath taken away my reproach:

And she called his name Joseph; and said, The LORD shall add to me another son.

Genesis 30:21-24

It is only after God's desire is fulfilled in our lives that our desire will be fulfilled. Rachel was able to have a child after

Leah had given birth to six children. In other words, our desire will only be fulfilled when we learn to fulfill God's desire first.

CHAPTER 8

THE DAY AFTER THE WORD OF PROMISE IS RELEASED

And it shall come to pass, if thou shalt hearken diligently unto the voice of the LORD thy God, to observe and to do all his commandments which I command thee this day, that the LORD thy God will set thee on high above all nations of the earth:

And all these blessings shall come on thee, and overtake thee, if thou shalt hearken unto the voice of the LORD thy God.

Deuteronomy 28:1-2

The day after the word of promise— the word of the Lord— is given is the beginning of responsibility for you. The individual receiving the word of promise has a great responsibility and a role to play in bringing the word of the Lord to pass. The responsibility is left for the individual to find.

When a word of promise is given to us, the first thing we must learn to do is to find out what role God wants us to play for the word of the Lord to come to pass. Many of us, after receiving a word, get thrilled and excited for the word. That is all right. However, after the excitement comes responsibility. That is the part we don't like. We don't like the word responsibility. We can go around boasting of the fanciful words given to us. We can say to friends or to our relatives, "See! God spoke to me through a man of God that I am going to become a great preacher, a great evangelist or that I am going to be rich and famous." Or, "I am going to have a big mansion and a lot of money." But we must remember that it is just a word of promise. It takes more than one person to bring a promise to pass. So when God, through a prophet or a man of God, gives you a "word of promise," you must participate in bringing the promise to pass.

Many times we are quick to find out God's role concerning the promise that is given to us, without finding out our roles. We say, "God, You promised two years ago that You are going to make me a great preacher or businessman, and yet it has not come to pass." We are very quick to point our fingers at God's responsibility instead of our own. The first thing we must look for or consider after a "word of promise" is given to us is our role, before God's role. God is

The Day After the Word of Promise is Released

and will always remain faithful to any "word of promise" given to us. We are the ones who are not faithful in our role.

When a "word of promise" is given to us, a covenant agreement is immediately set in motion. God provides a verbal covenant or agreement which says "This is what I am going to do for you." God is faithful in keeping His terms of the agreement. He will never be slack, nor will He negate His agreement. We are the ones who are slack and negate the agreement because of our failure to understand our role and responsibility in the agreement. A seed that is planted cannot effectively grow into a mature tree unless the farmer takes care of that seed. The farmer must water the seed. He must clear away the weeds around the seed to make sure that nothing prevents the seed from germinating or growing properly. You see, the farmer has a responsibility. If the farmer does not take care of the seed, then the seed will not grow to its full potential.

Every time we fail to maintain our responsibility, we break the covenant. Although we always blame God when the word of promise given to us fails to come to pass, what we need to do instead is to examine ourselves and see how we have responded to our role and responsibility. Did we keep the terms of the agreement? Did we water the seed? Did we clear away the weeds around the seed, or did we just allow the cares of this world to choke the "word of promise" given to us? These are some of the questions we must ask ourselves when "words" given to us are not coming to pass. We must shift the blame from God and from the man of God to examining ourselves. This is very important. It is so common these days. When a word of promise is given and it does not come to pass, the first thing we say is that the prophet must be a false prophet or a false man of God. While it is true that there are false prophets and false men of God, there are true prophets and true men of God. Even when a true man of God gives a word, if you do not play your role and find out your responsibility, it will still not come to pass. So instead of pointing your finger at God or at the men of God, let us start pointing the finger back at ourselves.

Let's look at the Scripture again in the book of Deuteronomy.

And it shall come to pass, if thou shalt hearken diligently unto the voice of the LORD thy God, to observe and to do all his commandments which I command thee this day, that the LORD thy God will set thee on high above all nations of the earth:

The Day After the Word of Promise is Released

And all these blessings shall come on thee, and overtake thee, if thou shalt hearken unto the voice of the LORD thy God.

Deuteronomy 28:1-2

We see that the key word here is that "it shall come to pass." What shall come to pass? The "word of promise" that is given to us. But there is a responsibility that we must uphold. There are things that we must do. We cannot just sit on our behinds and expect the promise given to us to manifest right before our eyes. The Scripture says that "if thou shalt hearken diligently unto the voice of the Lord, to observe and to do all his commandments... ." There is always an "if" when the "word of promise" is given. The "if" is the responsibility that we have to carry out. It is the role that we have to play. Many of us do not like the "ifs." We just want to see the promise coming to pass.

The Scripture went further to say that, even in carrying out our responsibility, we must carry it out diligently. The "t" must be crossed and the "i" dotted. The word "diligently" means the act of having or showing careful and sustained effort and application in what you are doing. It is being meticulous in what you are doing. In other words, we must be

Prophetic Development

careful, meticulous and show effort in carrying out our responsibility. Our responsibility must not be done haphazardly. We must be committed to it and be consistent with it.

Then "the Lord thy God will set thee on high.. ." High is where the promise is. It is where we always desire to be. But we must take care of our responsibility in order to be set on the high of our promise. Often we prefer to focus on the "and it shall come to pass...." We must learn to concentrate on the "if thou shalt hearken to the voice of the Lord." We must meditate on the "word of promise" given to us in order to find out what is expected of us. When a word is given to us, the first thing we must look for and be thrilled about should be what we need to do as given in the word. We should not just be thrilled with God's role and forget our role.

If when he seeth the sword come upon the land, he blow the trumpet, and warn the people;

Then whosoever heareth the sound of the trumpet, and taketh not warning; if the sword come, and take him away, his blood shall be upon his own head.

Ezekiel 33:3-4

The Day After the Word of Promise is Released

Look at what the Scripture says here. The Bible says that when a watchman– a prophet or a man of God– blows or sounds his trumpet concerning a danger, if the people who hear the sound of the trumpet refuse to obey the sound or take to the warning, "if the sword comes and takes him away, his blood shall be upon his own head." In other words, if the individual that is given a word of promise refuses to play his or her role or assume his or her responsibility, whatever happens to that individual will be his or her own fault and not the fault of the man of God.

For the LORD God is a sun and shield: the LORD will give grace and glory: no good thing will he withhold from them that walk uprightly.

Psalm 84:11

God promises that He will not withhold any good thing from us. What good thing? The word of promise He gave to us through the man of God. But there is a requirement that must be met for the "good thing" to come to pass. The person in need of the good thing must "walk uprightly." In other words, we must continually maintain a present tense righteousness. We must walk according to His precepts and be continually ready to observe His ways.

When a word of promise is given to us, weeks or months after it is given, we must learn to see the word of promise still fresh and new like we saw it when it was given to us.

The LORD's lovingkindnesses indeed never cease, For His compassions never fail. They are new every morning; Great is Thy faithfulness.

Lamentations 3:22-23 (NAS)

Daily, weekly, monthly and yearly the promise given to us must remain fresh in our hearts. We must cease from letting it get old and losing its value in our eyes. It must stay as valuable as it was when we received it. Often times Christians, after receiving a "word of promise" and seeing that it is not coming to pass in days, weeks, months or even years, lose their appreciation for the word of promise. They fail to respect, cherish and value the word that was given to them.

They go around looking for new "words of promise." They always like a new word and never do anything with their previous words. When the new "word of promise" does not come to pass in their time frame, they again immediately lose value for the promise. We must get out of this mindset.

The Day After the Word of Promise is Released

The promises of God are steadfast and real. They are renewed every morning. In other words, every morning they are re-polished to make them more attractive and new than the previous morning. This is what we need to do with the "words of promise" given to us. We need to polish those words with prayer, fasting and meditation to make them new in our sight every morning. A "word of promise" not cleaned and polished will be dusty and will not look new, and then it will not be appreciated.

A dusty table is never appreciated until it is cleaned. We must do the same thing concerning the dust over the "words of promise" that have been given to us.

Most of us have promises that have been covered with weeks, months and years worth of dust. We never bother to dust our promises. Once we realize that the promise or word given has not come to pass in the first week, we immediately dump those words under our beds, put them on our shelves and forget they are there. Then we go out in search of a new word, hoping that these new words or promises will be accomplished in the first week.

THE GIFT OF GOD WITHIN YOU

Neglect not the gift that is in thee, which was given thee by prophecy, with the laying on of the hands of the presbytery.

Meditate upon these things; give thyself wholly to them; that thy profiting may appear to all.

I Timothy 4:14-15

Paul was giving Timothy one of the greatest admonishments of our time. He told Timothy not to *neglect the gift* that is in him. What gift? The gift of the word of promise. The word of the Lord comes with a "gift." The gift is the word of promise that is given. When a man of God or a prophet gives a word of the Lord to you, the "word" that is given is a gift. We must not neglect the gift that is imparted to us. We must continually meditate on it and ponder it so that it can remain new and fresh inside of us.

STIRRING THE WORD OF PROMISE

Wherefore I put thee in remembrance that thou stir up the gift of God, which is in thee by the putting on of my hands.

II Timothy 1:6

The Day After the Word of Promise is Released

We need also to continually stir up in us the word of promise that is given to us. The word "stir up" is found only here in the New Testament. The verb is ANAZOPYREO. The prepositional prefix ANA has two meanings, "up" and "again." The middle item ZO means "life." The last root PYR means "fire." If we take ANA as "again," the full meaning then would be "stir alive again into a flame." It also means to "kindle to flame" or "to fan into a flame." Other meanings given to this word are "to stir up into a living flame" or "to keep at white heat." Paul admonished Timothy "to stir up the gift," not because Timothy had lost his early fire, but like every believer he needed an incentive to keep the early fire burning at full flame. The flame had not gone out, but it was burning slowly and had to be agitated to white heat. The tendency is for the fire of the word of promise given to us to go out. We must watch the fire on the altar of our heart. Anyone who has burned wood in a fireplace knows that periodically it is necessary to add fresh fuel, and sometimes to fan the embers into a flame. We need to keep alive the inner flame by adding the fuel of the Word of God and fanning it with prayer.

Therefore we ought to give the more earnest heed to the things which we have heard, lest at any time we should let them slip.

Hebrews 2:1

Paul here speaks about giving heed to the word we have received. The word "heed" in Greek means "to lean forward and pay very close attention so as to let nothing slip away, that nothing be wasted." When we receive a word from the Lord, we must pay very close attention with our spiritual hearts and ears. Often times, believers receive a word with such haphazardness and superficiality that the word is soon lost— just because they were not paying close attention to what the Lord said.

We need to treat the word of the Lord with great sensitivity and responsibility. When the word of the Lord is released to us, we become the stewards of the word of the Lord. We will have to answer to the Lord for what we have done with all the prophetic words and the quickened words that have come to us by the Holy Spirit. We must receive the Word of God with a good and honest heart, with humility and meekness, with careful attentiveness and finally as a Word of God, not of man. When we receive the prophetic word with these attitudes, the word will always become fruitful in our lives and move us on toward perfection. As we receive the word of the Lord, we are mandated to test the word that has been released into our lives. There is a divine principle found throughout Scripture concerning prophetic words. That is, the word is received, the word is tested, and then the word is fulfilled. Many believers would like to receive a dynamic word, bypass this middle stage of the testing of the word, and enter into that word without any persecution.

The thief cometh not, but for to steal, and to kill, and to destroy: I am come that they might have life, and that they might have it more abundantly.

John 10:10

Whenever the word of the Lord is released, whether it is a biblical word, a command, a promise or a prophetic word received into our lives as a promise, that word will be tested and tried and it will come to pass as we respond to the test. In John 10:10, the Lord teaches us the nature of the enemy that attacked us and the purpose of his attack. When we receive a word from the Lord, immediately the thief will come to try to steal the blessing and the promise that the Lord has given us. The devil is a thief and has been a thief from the beginning. He comes to steal anything he can pressure out of our lives, or that he can get us to throw away and say is not really from the Lord.

The word "thief" is defined as one who takes the goods or personal property of another without his knowledge or consent, without any intention of returning them. The enemy is truly a thief and he will come and take all spiritual properties and spiritual knowledge from you without your consent, if you do not protect the word that God gives you. The enemy has many ways of stealing the word of God from us. Often he throws discouragement our way, blow by blow, time after time. As we become worn down, our faith weakens. Without diligently and fervently applying our faith to the word, the word will never come to pass. He may come and rob the seed from our hearts before it has taken hold within our spirits, so that it never even develops.

> **Now the serpent was more subtil than any beast of the field which the LORD God had made. And he said unto the woman, Yea, hath God said, Ye shall not eat of every tree of the garden?**
>
> **Genesis 3:1**

The Day After the Word of Promise is Released

The enemy will throw confusion into your mind. Genesis 3 is an illustration of how the thief will come with confusion to steal the good word of God from our lives. The serpent or the devil is a very crafty being. He will use any craftiness he can think of that could destroy our lives. He delights in confusing us by twisting the word God gave us so that you begin questioning the word, or begin to think maybe you misunderstood it. In verse 1 the devil says, "Yea, hath God said?" This is the way the thief keeps after us. "Has God said? Did God really say that? Are you sure that this is what the Lord is going to do?" We must rebuke the devourer. We must close our ears to any twisting of the good word of God. We must not allow the thief to steal what God has given us in order to bring forth great things. When the prophetic word comes into our lives, we must hear it, pay close attention to what the Lord is saying and retain it. That is, make sure that it is planted deep within our hearts and then by persevering, by enduring, put our shoulders to the task. If we do these things, we will produce a good crop. But if we let the thief come in and steal the seed, there will be no crop at all.

That ye be not slothful, but followers of them who through faith and patience inherit the promises.

Hebrews 6:12

Prophetic Development

The Apostle here gives us two key New Testament words which must be acted upon in our lives. The qualities of "faith" and "patience" are prerequisites to inheriting the promise. Whenever the prophetic word comes to you, you must adhere to that word with faith. When we receive a word from God, that word must be united with faith in order for that word to profit us and to come to pass in our lives. There have been many instances of people receiving a prophetic word from the Lord, but who stumbled in disbelief. Through their own narrowness of mind and smallness of heart they have canceled the great promises of God.

> **This charge I commit unto thee, son Timothy, according to the prophecies which went before on thee, that thou by them mightest war a good warfare;**
>
> **I Timothy 1:18**

Whenever we receive a word of the Lord, we must understand that there will be a fight, a warfare, in order to bring that word to fulfillment. The Apostle Paul knew this and thus he exhorted his spiritual son Timothy to make certain he held on to the prophetic words that went over him. We must take all the prophecies that have gone over us and with them wage a mighty warfare of faith and patience to bring them to pass. Let us not be negligent. Let us not be slothful in enduring the afflictions and the trials that might come into our lives because of the word. We are in a long marathon that will have many obstacles and many challenges.

To request a complete catalog featuring books, video or audio tapes by Dr. John A. Tetsola, or to contact him for speaking engagements, please write or call:

Ecclesia Word Ministries International
P.O. Box 743
Bronx, New York 10462

(718) 904-8530
(718) 904-8107 fax
www.ecclesiaword.org
www.reformersministries.org
email: reformers@msn.com